"Law Enforcement Struggles"

Dedication

This book is dedicated to all the brave men and women who wear the badge, who face danger and adversity every day, and who sacrifice their own well-being to protect our communities.

You risk your lives to keep us safe, and your service goes far beyond the call of duty. To the fallen officers who gave their lives in the line of duty, you are not forgotten.

Your memory lives on in the hearts of those you served and in the unwavering commitment of those who carry on your legacy.

This book is also dedicated to the families of law enforcement officers, who stand by their side through thick and thin, offering unwavering love and support.

You are the backbone of our heroes, and your sacrifices are equally profound

Preface

As a seasoned law enforcement officer, I have spent years delving into the complex world of crime and justice.

Over the years, I have encountered countless stories of bravery, compassion, and sacrifice within the ranks of law enforcement.

However, I have also witnessed the immense challenges, the hidden struggles, and the human toll that this demanding profession often takes.

This book, "Law Enforcement Struggles," is a culmination of those experiences, a deep dive into the realities of life as a law enforcement officer, shedding light on the often-overlooked aspects of this critical role in our society.

It is not intended to be a glorification of law enforcement, nor is it a condemnation.

Rather, it is an honest and insightful look into the complex world of those who dedicate their lives to upholding the law, revealing the human side of the badge and the sacrifices they make to protect us all.

I hope this book will foster a deeper understanding and appreciation for the challenges faced by law enforcement officers, while also inspiring dialogue, reflection, and meaningful change within the profession.

Introduction

The thin blue line, a metaphor for the boundary between order and chaos, has been a symbol of law enforcement for generations.

But behind that line, a complex world exists, filled with both heroism and hardship.

This book delves into the often-overlooked realities of life as a law enforcement officer, exploring the financial, mental, and day-to-day challenges faced by both men and women working in the field.

From the pressures of dealing with crime and violence to the emotional toll of witnessing human suffering, "Law Enforcement Struggles" paints a raw and honest picture of the sacrifices and hardships officers endure.

It sheds light on the financial burdens of the profession, including low salaries and the cost of training and equipment, as well as the psychological impact of constant exposure to trauma and the need for a strong support system.

Through personal stories and insightful analysis, this book aims to foster a deeper understanding and appreciation for the sacrifices made by those who dedicate their lives to upholding the law.

It is a testament to their courage, resilience, and unwavering commitment to serving and protecting our communities.

By understanding the struggles faced by law enforcement officers, we can cultivate greater empathy, support, and ultimately, a more just and equitable society.

Chapter 1: The Thin Blue Line: A Glimpse into the Word of Law Enforcement

The Calling

The thin blue line—a phrase that evokes a sense of authority, protection, and the unwavering commitment to upholding the law. It's a line that separates order from chaos, safety from danger, and it's guarded by individuals who have dedicated their lives to serving and protecting their communities. But what compels a person to choose such a challenging and demanding career path? What drives them to put themselves in harm's way, to face the darkness that lurks in the shadows, to confront the very worst of humanity?

The answer lies in a complex tapestry woven from motivations, values, and a deep-seated desire to make a difference. For some, it's a calling, a sense of duty etched into their souls from a young age. They see law enforcement as a noble profession, a way to give back to their community, to be a beacon of hope in times of fear and despair. They yearn to protect the vulnerable, to stand as a bulwark against injustice, to be the voice for the voiceless. Their hearts beat with a rhythm of courage, their minds are sharp and analytical, and their spirits are fueled by a burning passion for justice.

Others are driven by a more personal experience—a tragic event that shaped their worldview, a moment of vulnerability that ignited a desire to help others avoid similar pain. Perhaps they witnessed the devastating consequences of crime firsthand, or they lost someone close to them due to violence. The scars of those experiences may linger, but they also fuel a determination to make a difference, to prevent others from suffering the same fate. They see law enforcement as a path to healing, a way to channel their own pain into a force for good.

For many, the decision to pursue a career in law enforcement is a family tradition, a legacy passed down through generations. They grew up surrounded by the stories of their parents, grandparents, or siblings who served with honor and distinction. They admire the courage and resilience of those who came before them, and they feel a profound sense of responsibility to uphold the family legacy. They see it as a way to honor their ancestors, to carry the torch of justice into the future.

The motivations are as diverse as the individuals who choose this profession, but they all share a common thread—a belief in the inherent goodness of humanity, a commitment to upholding the law, and a desire to make a promising impact on the world.

But the road to becoming a law enforcement officer is not paved with roses. It's a journey fraught with challenges and sacrifices, both visible and invisible. It's a journey that demands resilience, mental toughness, and a deep understanding of the complexities of human nature. It's a journey that requires unwavering dedication, a commitment to continuous learning, and a willingness to face the darkness without succumbing to its allure.

It's a journey that often pushes individuals to their limits, testing their physical and emotional strength, forcing them to confront the darkest aspects of humanity. It's a journey that requires an unyielding faith in the good, even when the world seems consumed by evil.

And yet, despite the challenges, those who choose this path often find themselves profoundly rewarded. They find meaning in their work, purpose in their actions, and a deep sense of camaraderie with those who share their commitment to justice. They find strength in their shared experiences, support in their common struggles, and a bond forged in the crucible of danger and sacrifice.

The thin blue line is not just a symbol of authority; it's a testament to the courage, resilience, and unwavering commitment of those who stand on its front lines. It's a reminder of the sacrifices they make, the dangers they face, and the difference they strive to make in the world. It's a symbol of hope in the face of darkness, a beacon of light in a world that often seems consumed by chaos. And it's a reminder that the fight for justice, for safety, for a better world, is a journey worth taking, no matter the cost.

The Oath

The oath taken by law enforcement officers is a solemn promise, a commitment to upholding the law and protecting citizens. It's a pledge that goes far beyond the words on a piece of paper; it's a vow to embody the ideals of justice, fairness, and public service. This oath represents a profound weight of responsibility, a burden that officers carry every day.

The oath often begins with a declaration of loyalty to the Constitution and the laws of the land. This commitment signifies a dedication to upholding the rule of law, regardless of personal beliefs or biases. Officers pledge to protect and serve all citizens, ensuring that everyone is treated with respect and dignity, regardless of their background, beliefs, or circumstances. They agree to enforce the law fairly and impartially, making decisions based on evidence and the law, not personal opinions.

This oath demands an unwavering commitment to ethical conduct, a steadfast resolve to uphold the highest standards of professionalism. Officers pledge to be honest, trustworthy, and accountable for their actions. They agree to treat all individuals with respect, even those who are accused of crimes. They are sworn to use their authority responsibly, with a commitment to protecting individual rights and freedoms.

The oath speaks to the inherent dangers of law enforcement, the risks officers face every day in the line of duty. They pledge to protect the public, even at personal risk, to be prepared to confront danger and violence in the pursuit of justice. This commitment requires immense courage, a willingness to put one's life on the line to safeguard the safety of others.

However, the oath also recognizes the complex and demanding nature of the job. It acknowledges the emotional toll, the psychological strain, and the potential for burnout. Officers pledge to remain vigilant, to be aware of their limitations, and to seek support when needed. They commit to maintaining their mental and emotional well-being, understanding that their ability to serve effectively depends on their own health and stability.

The oath is a constant reminder of the purpose and responsibility of law enforcement. It's a call to action, a commitment to upholding the law, protecting the innocent, and serving the public with honor and integrity. It's a daily reminder of the trust that is placed in them, the trust that they must earn and maintain through every interaction, every decision, and every action.

It's important to note that the oath is not just a theoretical concept; it's a lived reality for every law enforcement officer. Every day, they are faced with situations that test their commitment, their resolve, and their values. They must make difficult decisions, confront dangerous situations, and deal with the emotional weight of their work. The oath is a guiding principle, a moral compass that helps them navigate these challenging circumstances.

Personal stories and examples

To illustrate the weight of the oath, consider the story of Officer Jones, a young patrol officer in a small town. She had just graduated from the police academy, filled with enthusiasm and a desire to serve her community. The oath she took felt like a promise she was determined to uphold. But on her first night on patrol, she encountered a domestic violence call. The scene was chaotic, with yelling and fear in the air. Officer Jones had to use her training to de-escalate the situation, to protect the victim, and to ensure the safety of everyone involved. The experience left her shaken, but also filled with a sense of purpose. She had kept her oath, had acted with courage and compassion, and had made a real difference.

Or consider the story of Detective Smith, an experienced investigator working on a complex murder case. He had been on the force for over twenty years, had seen his share of violence and tragedy. But this case was different. The victim was a young child, and the suspect was a member of the community, someone Detective Smith knew. He felt a heavy weight on his shoulders, not just the pressure of solving the case, but the responsibility of ensuring justice for the victim and for the community. The oath he had taken years ago became a source of strength, a reminder of the importance of his work.

These are just two examples of the countless ways in which the oath is lived out by law enforcement officers every day. It's a constant reminder of the responsibility they bear, the sacrifices they make, and the commitment they have to uphold the law and protect citizens. It's a pledge that shapes their actions, their decisions, and their lives.

The oath and the public's trust

The oath taken by law enforcement officers is not just a personal commitment; it's also a pledge to the community they serve. It represents a promise of protection, of justice, and of upholding the rule of law. This promise builds trust, a foundation upon which a healthy and safe society can flourish.

However, this trust is fragile, easily eroded by misconduct, corruption, or a lack of transparency. When officers fail to uphold their oath, when they abuse their power or violate the public's trust, it has far-reaching consequences. It breeds cynicism, distrust, and fear, making it more difficult for law enforcement to do its job effectively.

The public's trust in law enforcement is essential for effective policing. It allows officers to do their job more effectively, to gain cooperation from citizens, and to build stronger relationships with the communities they serve. But this trust must be earned, nurtured, and constantly reinforced.

Beyond the oath: The ongoing conversation

While the oath is a powerful symbol of commitment and responsibility, it's not a guarantee of ethical conduct or effective policing. The realities of law enforcement are complex, demanding constant reflection, critical analysis, and a willingness to adapt and improve.

There's a need for ongoing dialogue about the challenges and opportunities facing law enforcement, a conversation that includes officers, community members, policymakers, and academics. This dialogue should focus on issues of accountability, transparency, diversity, and the evolving role of law enforcement in a rapidly changing world.

By embracing this ongoing conversation, by acknowledging the complexities of the job, and by striving to live up to the ideals enshrined in their oath, law enforcement officers can continue to build trust, promote justice, and ensure a safer and more equitable society for all.

The Reality

The reality of policing is far from the romanticized image often portrayed in movies and television. It's a demanding profession that requires a unique blend of physical and mental fortitude, unwavering dedication, and the ability to handle stressful and unpredictable situations with composure. Every day, officers face a multitude of challenges, ranging from routine patrols to life-or-death confrontations.

The day typically begins with a roll call, where officers receive their assignments, briefing notes, and updates on any ongoing investigations or incidents. The shift can range from eight to twelve hours, and officers are often on call 24/7, ready to respond to emergencies at a moment's notice.

A significant portion of an officer's time is spent on routine patrols, driving through assigned sectors, keeping an eye out for suspicious activity, and interacting with the public. These patrols are crucial for maintaining a visible presence, deterring crime, and building relationships with community members. However, routine patrols can be monotonous and sometimes dangerous, requiring officers to stay vigilant and prepared for anything.

Responding to calls is the heart of police work, and it's where officers encounter the full spectrum of human behavior, from mundane traffic violations to serious crimes. Each call presents a unique challenge, requiring quick thinking, sound judgment, and the ability to adapt to rapidly evolving situations. From domestic disputes and traffic accidents to burglaries, assaults, and even homicides, officers must navigate a vast array of situations, often under immense pressure and in high-risk environments.

The unpredictable nature of the job is one of its most defining characteristics. No two days are ever the same, and officers must be prepared to deal with anything at any time. One moment they might be assisting a stranded motorist, and the next, they could be responding to a hostage situation or a mass shooting. This constant uncertainty can be mentally taxing, requiring officers to maintain a high level of emotional resilience and a strong sense of mental fortitude.

Beyond the immediate dangers, the job of a law enforcement officer takes a toll on their mental health. They are constantly exposed to trauma, witnessing the worst of humanity, and grappling with the consequences of violence and crime. This exposure can lead to post-traumatic stress disorder (PTSD), anxiety, depression, and other mental health challenges. The emotional burden of the job can be overwhelming, and officers often struggle to find support and coping mechanisms.

Despite the inherent dangers and the emotional toll, law enforcement officers are driven by a sense of duty, a desire to serve and protect their communities. They face their challenges with courage, compassion, and a deep commitment to upholding the law and ensuring public safety. Their sacrifices are often unseen and underappreciated, yet they are the backbone of society, working tirelessly to keep our communities safe.

To illustrate the daily grind and unseen sacrifices, consider the following scenarios:

The Routine Patrol:

Officer Jones begins her shift with a routine patrol of her assigned district, a quiet suburban neighborhood. As she drives, she observes her surroundings, looking for any signs of criminal activity or suspicious behavior. She checks businesses for signs of forced entry, interacts with residents and business owners, and responds to minor traffic violations. While these tasks may seem mundane, they are crucial for maintaining order and deterring crime. Officer Jones also uses this time to build relationships with community members, becoming a familiar face in the neighborhood and fostering trust.

The Domestic Disturbance:

Officer Smith receives a call for a domestic disturbance at a nearby apartment complex. He arrives at the scene and is immediately confronted with a tense situation, with a screaming couple and a crowd of neighbors gathering outside. Officer Smith must quickly assess the situation, de-escalate the conflict, and ensure the safety of everyone involved. He carefully separates the couple and attempts to calm them down, using his training and experience to navigate the emotional turmoil. He interviews witnesses, gathers information, and ultimately determines that the situation does not warrant an arrest. However, the emotional impact of witnessing this domestic dispute lingers with him long after he leaves the scene.

The Fatal Accident:

 Officer Davis is dispatched to a fatal accident on a busy highway. As he approaches the scene, he is met with a chaotic and heartbreaking sight: a mangled car, emergency responders attending to the injured, and a family huddled together in shock and grief. Officer Davis must control the scene, ensuring the safety of everyone involved, while also providing support to the victims and their families. He must gather information, interview witnesses, and document the details of the accident. He faces the difficult task of informing the family of the deceased, a somber and emotionally draining experience.

These scenarios illustrate the variety of situations that officers face on a daily basis. They must be prepared for anything, from the mundane to the extraordinary, always ready to act quickly and decisively while maintaining their composure and professionalism.

Their work is not just about enforcing the law; it's about protecting lives, preserving peace, and serving as a source of support for their communities. Their sacrifices are often unseen, but their impact is profound. They work tirelessly to ensure our safety, often putting their own lives on the line without

hesitation. We should recognize and appreciate the sacrifices they make, for they are the thin blue line between order and chaos, safeguarding our communities and upholding the rule of law.

The Risk

The thin blue line, as it's often called, is a metaphor for the separation between order and chaos, between law and lawlessness. It's a line that law enforcement officers walk every day, a line that separates them from the very dangers they face. The job is not for the faint of heart. It demands courage, resilience, and a strong sense of duty. But the dangers are real, and they are ever-present. Every day, officers encounter individuals who have chosen to operate outside the bounds of the law, individuals who pose a threat to their safety and the safety of the public they serve.

From the moment they put on their uniform, officers are acutely aware of the risks they face. They may be called to a domestic disturbance where tempers are flaring and violence is a possibility. They might be sent to investigate a suspicious vehicle, never knowing if the occupants are armed or have malicious intent. They could find themselves in a high-speed chase, where a fleeing suspect is putting lives at risk. The unpredictability of the job is one of its most challenging aspects.

The threats officers face go beyond physical harm. They often witness acts of violence, trauma, and human suffering that leave lasting psychological scars. They are forced to confront the darkest aspects of human nature, seeing the very worst of society. They are tasked with dealing with individuals who are mentally unstable, addicted to drugs, or driven by desperation. Each encounter carries the potential for danger, and each officer must be prepared to react quickly and decisively.

The constant exposure to violence and danger takes a heavy toll on officers' mental and emotional well-being. The adrenaline rush that comes with confronting a dangerous situation can become addictive, blurring the lines between work and life. Many officers experience PTSD, anxiety, and depression as a result of their work. They struggle to separate the horrors they witness on the job from their personal lives, finding it difficult to relax and leave the stress behind.

The risks extend beyond the immediate threat of violence. Officers are often targets of retaliation from criminals they have apprehended or investigated. They may face threats of harm to themselves or their families, and they must be constantly vigilant about their safety. They learn to trust their instincts and rely on their training to assess potential threats, but the knowledge that danger is always lurking can be a constant source of anxiety.

The risks of the job are not always apparent to the public. The media often focuses on high-profile cases of officer-involved shootings or instances of police misconduct, perpetuating a negative perception of the profession. But the vast majority of law enforcement officers are dedicated to serving their communities and upholding the law. They are the ones who respond to calls for help, who put themselves in harm's way to protect others, and who work tirelessly to ensure the safety of their communities.

The risks they face are a testament to their bravery and commitment to their duty. They are the thin blue line that stands between order and chaos, and they deserve our respect, gratitude, and unwavering support.

It's important to acknowledge that law enforcement is a complex and often misunderstood profession. The dangers officers face are real, and they deserve our attention and understanding. The constant threat to their safety, both physical and emotional, should not be taken lightly. As we strive to improve the relationship between law enforcement and the communities they serve, we must recognize the sacrifices officers make and the risks they endure on a daily basis. Their dedication and courage deserve our respect and appreciation.

The Divide

The divide between law enforcement and the public is a complex and multifaceted issue that has been a source of tension and scrutiny for decades. This complex relationship is shaped by a myriad of factors, including historical events, societal perceptions, media portrayals, and personal experiences. At its core, it revolves around the fundamental concepts of trust and mistrust.

On one side of the divide stands law enforcement, often viewed as the guardians of public safety, tasked with upholding the law and protecting citizens. They are trained to enforce the rules, apprehend criminals, and ensure order within society. Their role is inherently demanding, requiring them to confront danger, make quick decisions under pressure, and often witness the worst aspects of human behavior. This constant exposure to violence, trauma, and moral ambiguity can shape their worldviews and lead to a sense of separation from the broader community.

The public, on the other side, vie"s la' enforcement through a lens shaped by their own experiences, cultural narratives, and media consumption. For some, law enforcement represents a symbol of protection, a source of comfort in times of crisis. They see officers as heroes, risking their lives to keep them safe and upholding justice. However, for others, the relationship with law enforcement is marked by fear, mistrust, and a history of negative interactions. They may have witnessed or experienced police brutality, racial profiling, or excessive force, leading to feelings of alienation and resentment.

This disconnect between public perception and the reality of law enforcement can manifest in various ways.

Media Portrayals:

News coverage of police brutality, misconduct, and controversial incidents can paint a negative picture of the profession, fueling mistrust and cynicism among the public.

Historical Events:

Historical events like the Civil Rights movement, the War on Drugs, and recent incidents of police shootings have highlighted systemic issues of racial bias, excessive force, and police brutality, leading to a deep-seated distrust of law enforcement within marginalized communities.

Lack of Transparency:

The public's lack of transparency into the inner workings of law enforcement, including police policies, disciplinary procedures, and investigations, can further exacerbate mistrust and fuel rumors and conspiracy theories.

Limited Interaction:

For many people, their only interaction with law enforcement is during a traffic stop, an arrest, or a stressful situation, which can create negative associations and reinforce existing biases.

Perceptions of Bias:

Perceptions of bias, both explicit and implicit, within law enforcement can lead to mistrust, particularly among minority groups who have historically been targeted by discriminatory policing practices.

Law Enforcement:

This divide presents significant challenges for both law enforcement and the public. It can lead to a breakdown in communication, a reluctance to cooperate with law enforcement, and a decrease in public safety. To bridge this divide, it is essential to foster dialogue, promote transparency, and build trust through genuine community engagement. This requires a commitment from both sides:

Embrace Transparency:

Openly sharing information about police policies, procedures, and investigations to build public trust and accountability.

Engage in Community Dialogue:

Actively participate in community forums, town halls, and community policing initiatives to build relationships, listen to concerns, and address issues head-on.

Promote Diversity and Inclusion:

Recruit and retain officers from diverse backgrounds to better reflect the communities they serve and foster trust and understanding.

Focus on De-escalation and Conflict Resolution:

Invest in training and resources for officers to de-escalate situations, use force as a last resort, and build positive interactions with the public.

Hold Officers Accountable:

Uphold strict accountability standards for officers, investigate allegations of misconduct promptly and thoroughly, and implement disciplinary measures when necessary.

Engage in Dialogue:

Participate in community meetings, town halls, and dialogues with law enforcement to share concerns and perspectives.

Promote Understanding:

Educate themselves about the challenges and complexities of law enforcement, dispel myths and misinformation, and support efforts to improve police-community relations.

Support Law Enforcement When Appropriate:

Recognize and acknowledge the value of law enforcement in protecting public safety and upholding the law.

Hold Law Enforcement Accountable:

Report misconduct and advocate for systemic changes to improve police practices and ensure accountability.

The Public:

Bridging the divide between law enforcement and the public is a long-term effort that requires a sustained commitment from both sides. It is not a task that can be accomplished overnight, but it is a necessary one for building a safer and more just society. By fostering understanding, promoting transparency, and actively engaging in dialogue, we can move towards a future where law enforcement and the public work together to build trust and create a more equitable and peaceful society.

Chapter 2: The Emotional Toll: Coping with Stress and Trauma

The Weight of Witnessing Trauma

The human mind is a remarkable instrument, capable of processing immense amounts of information and adapting to a wide range of experiences. Yet, even the strongest minds can be overwhelmed by the sheer volume of trauma, violence, and suffering that law enforcement officers regularly encounter. While they are trained to handle dangerous situations and maintain composure in the face of adversity, the psychological impact of witnessing such events cannot be underestimated.

The job demands officers to be emotionally detached, to compartmentalize their emotions and separate themselves from the pain and suffering they witness. This emotional armor, while necessary for survival in the line of duty, can also become a barrier to their own well-being. The constant exposure to trauma and violence can take a heavy toll, leading to a wide range of psychological issues, including post-traumatic stress disorder (PTSD).

PTSD is a mental health condition that can develop after a person has experienced or witnessed a traumatic event. Symptoms can include flashbacks, nightmares, avoidance of situations that remind them of the trauma, difficulty concentrating, and emotional numbness. For law enforcement officers, the triggers for PTSD can be numerous, from witnessing a fatal car accident to responding to a domestic violence call. The cumulative effect of multiple traumatic experiences can further amplify the risk of developing PTSD.

One of the most challenging aspects of PTSD for law enforcement officers is the feeling of isolation. In a profession where emotional vulnerability is often discouraged, seeking help can feel like a sign of weakness. This stigma surrounding mental health issues within law enforcement can prevent officers from acknowledging their struggles and seeking the treatment they need.

The emotional toll on officers can manifest in various ways. Some may experience increased irritability, anger, and difficulty controlling their emotions. Others may struggle with anxiety, depression, and feelings of hopelessness. These emotional struggles can have a significant impact on their personal lives, affecting their relationships with family, friends, and colleagues.

The stress and trauma experienced on the job can also lead to physical health problems. Officers may experience chronic pain, fatigue, sleep disturbances, and digestive issues. The constant adrenaline surges and heightened stress levels can take a toll on their cardiovascular health, increasing the risk of heart disease and stroke.

Recognizing the psychological impact of the job and breaking down the stigma surrounding mental health is crucial for supporting officers' well-being. Law enforcement agencies have a responsibility to provide their officers with access to mental health services and resources, creating a culture where seeking help is encouraged and supported.

Furthermore, officers themselves need to be proactive in taking care of their mental health. This includes engaging in healthy coping mechanisms such as exercise, mindfulness, and relaxation techniques. It's also essential for officers to develop strong support systems outside of work, connecting with loved ones, friends, and fellow officers who can provide understanding and support.

The emotional burden of witnessing trauma and violence is a significant reality for law enforcement officers. It is essential to acknowledge the psychological impact of the job, address the stigma surrounding mental health, and provide officers with the resources they need to maintain their well-being. By doing so, we can ensure that those who dedicate their lives to protecting our communities have the support they need to navigate the emotional challenges of their profession.

The Isolation of the Badge

The blue uniform, the badge, the authority—these are the outward symbols of the profession. Yet, beneath the surface lies a hidden world, one where emotional vulnerability is often discouraged, and the weight of stress and trauma can be isolating and overwhelming. Finding support and connection becomes an uphill battle in a profession where stoicism is often celebrated over emotional expression.

Imagine yourself as a rookie officer, fresh out of the academy, eager to make a difference. You're thrown into the reality of the streets, encountering violence, trauma, and human suffering on a daily basis. You're expected to be strong, to handle the pressure, to remain composed, even in the face of unspeakable horrors. This constant pressure can take a toll, chipping away at your emotional resilience. The fear, the adrenaline, the sense of responsibility—it all builds up, making it difficult to find solace in the very people you work with.

The "blue wall," that strong sense of brotherhood and sisterhood that is often touted as a positive aspect of law enforcement, can also become a barrier to seeking help. There's a fear of appearing weak, of being judged, of being labeled as unfit for the job. The pressure to conform to this rigid ideal of the stoic officer can lead to a dangerous cycle of isolation, where officers struggle to process their experiences and emotions, leaving them feeling alone and misunderstood.

The lack of readily available mental health resources within law enforcement exacerbates this issue. Many officers are afraid to seek help, fearing that it will jeopardize their careers. The stigma surrounding mental health issues within law enforcement is deeply ingrained, leading to a culture where officers are reluctant to admit vulnerability or seek the support they need.

This isolation isn't just about emotional wellbeing; it also impacts the officer's overall performance and health. When officers struggle to cope with stress and trauma, their decision-making abilities, their communication skills, and their ability to build rapport with the community can all suffer. The ripple effect extends beyond the individual officer, ultimately impacting public safety and the effectiveness of the law enforcement agency as a whole.

The need for support systems becomes critical in this context. Family, friends, and fellow officers can play an invaluable role in providing a safe space for officers to vent, to share their experiences, and to find support. However, building these support networks can be challenging, especially when officers are often isolated from their families due to shift work and the demands of the job.

It's not just about having a support system; it's also about fostering a culture within law enforcement that encourages emotional vulnerability and prioritizes mental health. This means creating a space where officers feel safe to talk about their experiences, to express their emotions, and to seek help without fear of judgment or reprisal.

The solution isn't simply about providing mental health services; it's about creating a fundamental shift in the culture of law enforcement, where vulnerability is embraced, and seeking help is not seen as a sign of weakness but as a sign of strength. Only then can we begin to address the emotional toll on officers, breaking the cycle of isolation and fostering a healthier and more supportive environment for those who dedicate their lives to protecting our communities.

Beyond the immediate needs of individual officers, there is a broader societal responsibility at play. We, as members of the community, must actively work to dismantle the stigma surrounding mental health, particularly within law enforcement. This includes encouraging open dialogue, educating ourselves about the realities of the profession, and advocating for better mental health resources and support systems.

By understanding the emotional struggles faced by law enforcement officers, we can move towards a more compassionate and supportive approach to policing. It's a journey that requires both individual and collective effort, a journey that necessitates a shift in mindset and a commitment to fostering a culture of care and respect for those who serve and protect.

The Stigma of Mental Health

The blue line, a symbol of strength and protection, often becomes a barrier to officers seeking help for their own struggles. The stigma surrounding mental health in law enforcement is a pervasive and deeply rooted issue. This stigma is fueled by a culture of stoicism, where vulnerability is seen as weakness, and seeking help can be perceived as a sign of failure. This creates a vicious cycle, where officers struggling with mental health issues are reluctant to come forward for fear of being judged, ostracized, or even disciplined. The consequences of this silence can be devastating, leading to burnout, substance abuse, and even suicide.

A common misconception is that law enforcement officers are inherently strong and resilient, capable of handling any stress or trauma they encounter. This misconception ignores the very real human cost of the job, the constant exposure to violence, death, and human suffering. Officers, like everyone else, are susceptible to the psychological impacts of trauma, and neglecting these impacts can lead to serious consequences.

The "thin blue line" mentality, while fostering a sense of camaraderie and shared purpose, can also create an environment of secrecy and silence. This can be particularly harmful for officers experiencing mental health challenges, as they may fear that seeking help will be seen as a betrayal of the code of brotherhood or sisterhood. This fear can prevent them from reaching out to colleagues, superiors, or mental health professionals, leaving them feeling isolated and alone in their struggles.

Several factors contribute to the stigma surrounding mental health in law enforcement:

Fear of Stigma:

Officers are often afraid of being labeled as weak, unstable, or unfit for duty if they seek mental health help. This fear can stem from a deeply ingrained belief within the law enforcement culture that seeking help is a sign of weakness and could jeopardize their career.

Fear of Retaliation:

Some officers worry that seeking help could result in disciplinary action, being ostracized by their colleagues, or even losing their jobs. This fear can be particularly prevalent in departments with a history of negative attitudes towards mental health issues.

Lack of Resources and Support:

Many departments lack adequate mental health resources and support for their officers. This lack of access can make it difficult for officers to get the help they need, further reinforcing the stigma and discouraging them from seeking assistance.

Limited Training and Awareness:

Training on mental health issues and stress management is often insufficient or lacking altogether in law enforcement. This lack of training can contribute to a lack of awareness and understanding of mental health challenges, making it harder for officers to recognize and address their own needs.

Cultural Norms and Expectations:

Law enforcement culture often places a premium on stoicism, resilience, and emotional control. This can create an environment where officers feel pressured to suppress their emotions and avoid seeking help.

The consequences of this stigma on officers' mental health and well-being are significant. They include:

Increased Rates of Mental Illness:

Law enforcement officers have significantly higher rates of mental health issues, including post-traumatic stress disorder (PTSD), anxiety, and depression, compared to the general population.

Substance Abuse:

The high stress and trauma associated with the job can lead to substance abuse as a coping mechanism. This can have devastating consequences on officers' lives, both professionally and personally.

Suicide:

Law enforcement officers are at a higher risk of suicide than the general population. The stigma surrounding mental health can contribute to this tragedy, preventing officers from seeking help and support when they need it most.

Burnout and Fatigue:

The constant exposure to stress and trauma can lead to burnout, job dissatisfaction, and fatigue. This can affect officers' performance, their relationships with colleagues and the public, and their overall well-being.

The barriers to seeking help and treatment for mental health issues in law enforcement are complex and multifaceted. They arise from a combination of cultural norms, systemic issues, and the lack of awareness and resources. It is imperative to address these barriers head-on to ensure that officers have access to the support and care they need to maintain their mental well-being.

Here are some steps that can be taken to address the stigma surrounding mental health in law enforcement:

Promote Open Dialogue:

Departments should create a culture where mental health is openly discussed and destigmatized. This can be achieved by encouraging officers to talk about their mental health, providing training and resources on mental health issues, and creating a safe space for officers to seek help without fear of judgment or retaliation.

Increase Resources and Support:

Departments should invest in adequate mental health resources, such as access to mental health professionals, peer support programs, and confidential counseling services. This ensures that officers have the resources they need to address their mental health needs effectively.

Improve Training and Awareness:

Mandatory training on mental health issues, stress management, and trauma-informed care should be a standard part of law enforcement training. This will increase awareness, understanding, and empathy for officers and their mental health needs.

Promote Leadership Support:

Leaders in law enforcement should set the tone by openly acknowledging and addressing mental health issues. They should demonstrate a commitment to creating a supportive and understanding environment for officers struggling with mental health challenges.

Challenge the Culture of Stoicism:

Departments need to move away from the traditional culture of stoicism and encourage officers to seek help when they need it. This involves challenging the perception that vulnerability is weakness and promoting a culture of support and compassion.

Promote Early Intervention:

Identifying and addressing mental health issues early on is crucial. Departments should implement programs that encourage officers to seek help proactively, such as stress management workshops, peer support groups, and confidential screening tools.

Provide Support for Families:

The mental health of officers can also impact their families. Departments should provide resources and support for families of officers, including education on mental health issues and access to support groups.

Advocate for Policy Changes:

Lawmakers and policymakers need to recognize and address the mental health needs of law enforcement officers. This can involve providing financial support for mental health resources, implementing policies that protect officers from discrimination for seeking help, and investing in research and training.

By addressing the stigma surrounding mental health and removing the barriers to seeking help, law enforcement agencies can create a culture of care and support that prioritizes the well-being of their officers. This not only benefits officers' individual mental health but also contributes to a safer and more effective law enforcement profession.

The Power of Resilience

The path to resilience is not a solitary one. Building coping mechanisms and strategies requires a multi-faceted approach, a combination of internal strength and external support. It's about equipping yourself with the tools to weather the storms of stress and trauma, while also seeking out safe harbors of understanding and support.

Mindfulness and Meditation:

The constant exposure to adrenaline-fueled situations can create a state of perpetual hypervigilance, leaving little space for rest and rejuvenation. Mindfulness and meditation techniques provide a counterbalance to this. They offer a way to anchor yourself in the present moment, to observe your thoughts and emotions without judgment. By focusing on your breath and cultivating a sense of calm, you can learn to navigate stressful situations with a greater sense of awareness and control.

Physical Exercise and Healthy Habits:

A healthy body is the foundation of a healthy mind. Regular physical exercise, whether it's running, weightlifting, or yoga, helps release endorphins, reduces stress hormones, and improves overall well-being. Adopting healthy eating habits, getting enough sleep, and avoiding alcohol and substance abuse are equally important for maintaining physical and mental resilience.

Cognitive Behavioral Therapy (CBT):

CBT is a type of therapy that helps individuals identify and challenge negative thought patterns and behaviors that contribute to stress and anxiety. It focuses on understanding the connection between thoughts, feelings, and behaviors, and on developing more adaptive ways of thinking and responding to situations. CBT can be particularly helpful in addressing the lingering effects of trauma and in developing coping mechanisms for future stressful encounters.

Support Groups and Peer Counseling:

Sharing your experiences with others who understand the unique pressures of law enforcement can provide immense relief. Support groups, such as those offered by the Law Enforcement Assistance Administration (LEAA) or other organizations, offer a safe space to connect with peers, share stories, and receive empathy and support. Peer counseling programs, where officers can talk to trained colleagues, can offer an informal yet valuable source of support.

Professional Counseling and Therapy:

Seeking professional help from a therapist or counselor is a sign of strength, not weakness. A therapist can provide a safe and confidential space to explore your experiences, work through trauma, and develop healthy coping mechanisms. They can also help you identify potential mental health concerns, such as PTSD or depression, and guide you toward appropriate treatment.

Taking Time Off:

The need for downtime is often overlooked in the demanding world of law enforcement. It is essential to prioritize rest and relaxation, taking time off for vacations, hobbies, or simply spending time with loved ones. These moments allow you to recharge, replenish your mental energy, and return to work with renewed focus and resilience.

Creating a Strong Support System:

The importance of a strong support system cannot be overstated. Surround yourself with people who understand the challenges you face, who offer unconditional love and support, and who encourage you to prioritize your well-being. This could include family, friends, colleagues, or even a mentor who has navigated similar challenges.

Engaging in Healthy Hobbies:

Pursuing hobbies and interests outside of work can provide a much-needed escape from the stresses of the job. These activities can help you relax, de-stress, and connect with your passions. Whether it's reading, painting, playing music, or spending time in nature, finding activities that bring you joy can significantly contribute to your overall well-being.

Finding Meaning and Purpose:

One of the most powerful sources of resilience comes from finding meaning and purpose in your work. Remembering the positive impact you have on your community, the lives you save, and the injustices you help to correct can provide a sense of fulfillment that fuels your motivation and helps you persevere through difficult times.

Developing a Sense of Humor:

Humor can be a potent antidote to stress. Learning to laugh at yourself, to find the lighter side of situations, and to share humor with colleagues can help lighten the load and foster a sense of camaraderie.

Building resilience is an ongoing process, requiring constant effort and attention. It's not a one-size-fits-all approach; it's about finding the strategies that work best for you and making them part of your daily routine. Remember, you are not alone. There are resources and support systems available to help you navigate the emotional challenges of law enforcement and to maintain your mental well-being.

The Importance of Support Systems

The emotional toll of law enforcement is a constant companion, and navigating those challenging waters requires a strong support system. This is where the importance of family, friends, and fellow officers comes into play. These relationships provide a vital lifeline for officers, offering a space for vulnerability, understanding, and the crucial emotional support that can help them cope with the inherent stresses of the job.

Think of it like this: Imagine a ship sailing through a turbulent sea. The ship represents an officer, navigating the unpredictable and often dangerous waters of law enforcement. The waves represent the stressors and traumas they face daily. But a strong support system acts as the anchor, providing stability and grounding, preventing the ship from being completely tossed about by the tempestuous sea.

For officers, family can offer a haven from the demanding world of policing. They provide an unconditional love and acceptance that can help officers de-stress, recharge, and find solace. Spouses and children, understanding the nature of the profession, can be a source of comfort and encouragement. They might not fully grasp the intricacies of the job, but their simple presence and love can make a world of difference.

Friends, especially those outside of law enforcement, offer a different perspective. They can provide a valuable outlet for officers to vent, share their experiences, and find a sense of normalcy. These relationships remind officers that they are not defined solely by their badge, allowing them to embrace their individuality and enjoy life outside of the demanding work environment.

Fellow officers, having experienced the same trials and tribulations, understand the unique challenges of the job. This shared understanding can create a powerful bond, fostering a sense of camaraderie and support. They can provide advice, offer an empathetic ear, and help each other navigate difficult situations. However, it's crucial to recognize that even within the "blue wall," maintaining healthy boundaries and seeking support from various sources is essential.

Unfortunately, the culture of law enforcement often discourages vulnerability and seeking help. This can lead to feelings of isolation and make officers hesitant to open up, even to their fellow officers. This is where creating a safe space for vulnerability becomes critical. It's about encouraging open communication, breaking down the stigma surrounding mental health, and fostering a culture that prioritizes well-being.

Imagine a scenario where a young officer is struggling with a particularly traumatic event. They feel overwhelmed and alone, but the fear of judgment or being perceived as weak prevents them from seeking help. This is where having a strong support system becomes paramount. A supportive friend, a trusted colleague, or a family member could provide a listening ear, offer comfort, and encourage the officer to seek professional help.

Building a strong support system involves actively cultivating meaningful relationships. It's about nurturing those connections, being present for others, and offering support in return. It also means recognizing the importance of seeking professional help when needed. Mental health resources should be readily available, and the stigma associated with seeking help needs to be addressed head-on.

Remember, even the most resilient officers need a safe harbor, a place to anchor themselves, and a network of support to weather the storms they encounter. Building strong relationships with family, friends, and colleagues can be the difference between navigating those storms and being overwhelmed by them. It's about fostering a culture of understanding, empathy, and support, allowing officers to face the emotional challenges of their work with greater strength and resilience.

Chapter 3: The Financial Struggle: The Cost of Serving and Protecting

The Low Pay Paradox

The low salaries paid to law enforcement officers stand in stark contrast to the significant risks and responsibilities they bear. This financial disparity creates a paradox, where those who dedicate their lives to public safety often struggle to secure their own financial well-being. While the public often values the service of law enforcement, the reality is that their salaries often fail to reflect the demanding nature of the job and the sacrifices they make.

Imagine a young officer fresh out of the academy, eager to serve and protect. They've invested years in training, undergone rigorous physical and mental tests, and dedicated themselves to upholding the law. Yet, they're likely to start with a salary that barely covers the basics of living. This financial strain can be a heavy burden, especially considering the high cost of living in many areas.

This is not just a problem for newly minted officers. Even seasoned veterans, with years of experience and expertise, often struggle to make ends meet. The financial pressures can be overwhelming, especially when officers are facing escalating costs of training, equipment, and personal expenses. The constant need to upgrade equipment, pay for specialized training, and even cover the costs of travel and overtime work can quickly deplete their limited earnings.

The financial disparity between the risks and responsibilities of the job and the compensation received creates a significant burden. It can lead to feelings of resentment, disillusionment, and a sense of being undervalued.

The low salaries paid to law enforcement officers have several negative consequences, both for the individual officers and for the communities they serve:

Recruitment and Retention Issues:

The low pay and financial strain make it difficult to attract and retain qualified individuals, leading to shortages of officers. This can impact the effectiveness and efficiency of police departments, as well as the overall safety and security of communities.

Increased Stress and Burnout:

The financial strain adds to the already high levels of stress and burnout experienced by law enforcement officers. Financial worries can distract from their duties, impair their judgment, and increase the risk of mental health problems.

Potential for Corruption:

When officers are struggling financially, they may be more susceptible to bribery or other forms of corruption, as they seek to supplement their income. This can erode public trust and undermine the integrity of law enforcement.

Limited Career Opportunities:

The low salaries can also limit career opportunities for law enforcement officers, making it difficult for them to advance in their field or pursue further education. This can create a sense of stagnation and limit the professional growth of officers.

The financial struggle faced by law enforcement officers is a complex issue with deep-rooted causes. It's a product of a complex interplay of factors, including:

Public Funding and Priorities:

Funding for law enforcement agencies is often limited, and public priorities can shift, impacting the allocation of resources. This can result in budget cuts that affect officer salaries and benefits.

Political Influence and Lobbying:

Political decisions, often influenced by lobbying groups, can shape funding allocations and salary levels for law enforcement.

The Value of Public Service:

The public often expresses appreciation for law enforcement officers, but this appreciation doesn't always translate into adequate financial support for the profession.

Addressing the financial struggles of law enforcement officers requires a multi-pronged approach:

Increase Salaries:

Law enforcement agencies should advocate for increased salaries that reflect the risks and responsibilities of the job. This requires a shift in public perception and a commitment to adequately funding law enforcement.

Reduce Costs:

Efforts should be made to reduce the hidden costs of the job, such as training, equipment, and personal expenses. This might involve providing more affordable training programs, offering equipment subsidies, or establishing financial assistance programs to help officers offset these expenses.

Improve Benefits:

Beyond salaries, law enforcement officers need access to comprehensive benefits, including health insurance, retirement plans, and paid leave. These benefits can contribute to their overall financial security and well-being.

Promote Financial Literacy:

Law enforcement agencies should provide training and resources on financial literacy to help officers manage their finances, plan for retirement, and avoid debt.

Advocate for Change:

Law enforcement officers need to advocate for their own rights and interests, working with policymakers and the public to create a more equitable and financially sustainable system.

The financial struggles faced by law enforcement officers are not simply a matter of personal responsibility. They are a consequence of systemic issues that require systemic solutions. It's time to recognize the sacrifices made by those who serve and protect, and to ensure that they are adequately compensated for their dedication and service. By addressing the financial disparity and creating a more equitable system, we can support the well-being of law enforcement officers and strengthen the bonds of trust between law enforcement and the communities they serve.

The Hidden Cost of the Badge

The "hidden costs" of the badge extend far beyond the standard paycheck. Law enforcement officers, often dedicated to serving and protecting, find themselves grappling with a financial reality that often goes unnoticed by the public. The financial burdens they carry, though often invisible, are a significant factor in their lives, impacting their well-being and potentially even their ability to continue serving. This subsection delves into these often overlooked financial burdens, exploring the costs of training, equipment, and personal expenses that weigh heavily on law enforcement officers.

The Cost of Training: Investing in Knowledge and Skills

Becoming a law enforcement officer requires a substantial investment in training and education. This investment begins with rigorous academy training, which includes extensive coursework, physical fitness requirements, and firearms proficiency. The cost of these academies can vary significantly, ranging from several thousand to tens of thousands of dollars, depending on the state and the type of law enforcement agency. While some academies may offer scholarships or tuition assistance, many officers find themselves shouldering a considerable financial burden to acquire the skills necessary for their profession.

Beyond the initial academy training, law enforcement officers face a continuous need for ongoing education and training. They must stay abreast of evolving laws, procedures, and tactics, requiring them to attend specialized courses, conferences, and workshops throughout their careers. These additional training programs can come with their own costs, including travel, accommodation, and course fees, further adding to the financial strain on officers.

Equipment Expenses: Essential Tools of the Trade

The "tools of the trade" for law enforcement officers often come with a hefty price tag. From basic equipment like uniforms, boots, and protective gear to more specialized tools like handcuffs, pepper spray, and firearms, the cost of maintaining a fully equipped officer can be significant. Many departments provide some basic equipment, but officers often find themselves having to purchase additional gear to enhance their safety and effectiveness. This can include items like bulletproof vests, high-quality boots, and specialized tactical gear, which can easily run into hundreds or even thousands of dollars.

The cost of firearms and ammunition is a particularly significant expense for law enforcement officers. While some departments provide firearms, many officers are required to purchase their own weapons. The cost of a quality firearm can easily range from several hundred to several thousand dollars, depending on the make and model. Ammunition expenses can add up quickly, especially for officers who engage in regular training or target practice to maintain proficiency.

Personal Expenses: The Hidden Costs of the Job

Beyond the costs of training and equipment, there are a number of personal expenses that often burden law enforcement officers. These expenses can include:

Vehicle expenses:

Officers often drive their personal vehicles to and from work and even during patrol duties. This leads to increased wear and tear on their vehicles, higher maintenance costs, and potentially higher insurance premiums. Some departments provide vehicles for patrol duty, but officers may still be required to use their personal vehicles for other work-related activities, like attending court hearings or transporting prisoners.

Childcare:

Shift work and irregular schedules often make it difficult for law enforcement officers to find affordable and reliable childcare. The cost of childcare can be a significant financial burden, especially for officers with young children.

Health insurance:

While some departments offer health insurance benefits, the cost of health insurance can be substantial, particularly for officers with families. Deductibles, co-pays, and out-of-pocket expenses can add up quickly, impacting officers' overall financial stability.

Mental health care:

The stress and trauma associated with the job often lead to mental health challenges for officers. While some departments offer mental health resources, these services may have limitations or require co-pays, leaving officers with a significant financial burden to access the care they need.

The Impact on Officers' Financial Well-being

These hidden costs can significantly impact the financial well-being of law enforcement officers. They can contribute to financial stress, limit career advancement, and even lead to officers leaving the profession. Officers may find themselves struggling to make ends meet, unable to afford basic necessities or to save for retirement. They may also be forced to work overtime or take on second jobs to supplement their income, further impacting their work-life balance and overall well-being.

The financial burdens faced by law enforcement officers are a significant concern that deserves greater attention and support. By understanding these hidden costs, we can better appreciate the sacrifices officers make and advocate for policies that provide them with fair compensation and adequate resources to meet their financial needs.

Solutions and Strategies for Addressing Financial Burdens

While the financial struggles faced by law enforcement officers are complex, there are several potential solutions and strategies that can help alleviate the burden:

Increased salaries and benefits:

Law enforcement officers deserve fair compensation that reflects the risks and responsibilities of their profession. Increased salaries and improved benefits, including health insurance, retirement plans, and paid time off, can help officers achieve financial security and reduce their stress levels.

Financial literacy programs:

Providing officers with access to financial literacy programs and resources can empower them to make informed financial decisions, manage their finances effectively, and plan for their future. These programs can cover topics like budgeting, debt management, saving, and investing.

Assistance with equipment expenses:

Departments can provide more support with equipment expenses by supplying officers with essential gear and offering discounts on specialized equipment. This can help reduce the financial burden on officers and ensure they have access to the tools they need to perform their duties effectively.

Childcare assistance:

Departments can provide assistance with childcare expenses by offering subsidized childcare programs or partnering with local organizations that provide affordable childcare services. This can help officers balance their work and family responsibilities and reduce their financial stress.

Mental health support:

Departments should prioritize mental health support for officers by providing access to confidential counseling services, mental health screenings, and resources for managing stress and trauma. This can help officers address their mental health needs without facing a significant financial burden.

By addressing these financial burdens, we can create a more supportive environment for law enforcement officers and help them achieve greater financial security. This will not only benefit officers and their families but also enhance their overall well-being and their ability to serve and protect our communities.

The Burden of Debt

The financial strain on law enforcement officers often extends beyond their modest salaries. It's a complex web of debt accumulated during their education, the high cost of living, and the constant need for professional development. The weight of student loans, mortgages, and other financial obligations adds to the already significant stress of the job. Many officers find themselves juggling multiple jobs or working overtime just to make ends meet, while still trying to manage their household expenses.

The decision to pursue a career in law enforcement is often driven by a strong sense of duty and a desire to serve the community. However, for many, the financial reality of the profession can be a harsh awakening. The pay for law enforcement officers varies significantly by jurisdiction, but it's widely acknowledged that salaries often don't reflect the risks and responsibilities associated with the job. This disparity between public service and financial security can leave officers feeling undervalued and financially insecure.

Higher education is often a requirement for law enforcement positions. In many states, an associate's or bachelor's degree is now a prerequisite for entry-level officer roles. This means that aspiring officers must often take on substantial student loan debt to acquire the necessary education, adding to their financial burdens right from the start of their careers. Even after graduating, officers often face ongoing expenses for specialized training, certifications, and professional development courses, further straining their budgets.

The cost of living has risen dramatically in recent years, and officers are not immune to these pressures. Housing costs, particularly in urban areas where many police departments are located, are a significant financial drain. Many officers find themselves struggling to afford rent or a mortgage, especially with the additional expenses of maintaining a family. Furthermore, the unpredictable nature of shift work and the need to be available for emergency calls can make it difficult to secure stable housing arrangements.

The financial burden can also extend beyond basic necessities. Officers frequently face unexpected expenses related to their work. This can include the cost of personal equipment, such as firearms, bulletproof vests, and uniforms, which can be quite costly. The constant exposure to potentially dangerous situations often necessitates the purchase of additional safety gear, further impacting personal finances.

The financial anxieties and pressures can have a significant impact on the well-being of law enforcement officers. The constant worry about money can exacerbate the stress and trauma they experience on the job, leading to feelings of anxiety, depression, and even burnout. This financial strain can also impact their personal relationships, as they may be forced to work extra shifts or take on second jobs to make ends meet, leaving little time for family and friends.

While the financial struggles faced by law enforcement officers are a serious concern, there are steps that can be taken to address these challenges. One crucial step is to advocate for fair compensation and benefits for officers. Lawmakers and policymakers must recognize the risks and sacrifices officers make and ensure that their salaries are commensurate with the responsibilities they shoulder.

Another important strategy is to promote financial literacy among law enforcement officers. Providing officers with access to resources and education on budgeting, financial planning, and debt management can help them manage their finances more effectively and alleviate some of the financial stress they experience.

The financial well-being of law enforcement officers is not just a personal issue; it has a direct impact on public safety. When officers are struggling financially, it can affect their focus, their ability to perform their duties effectively, and their overall mental and physical health. Addressing the financial challenges faced by law enforcement officers is an essential step towards ensuring a safer and more secure society.

The Importance of Financial Literacy

Financial literacy is a critical aspect of a law enforcement officer's life, often overlooked amidst the demanding nature of the profession. While serving and protecting, it is equally essential to protect one's financial well-being and plan for a secure future. Unfortunately, many officers find themselves burdened by financial challenges, including low salaries, high expenses, and a lack of financial education. This section aims to shed light on the importance of financial literacy for law enforcement officers, providing practical tips and resources for managing finances and planning for their future.

The Importance of Financial Literacy:

Understanding Your Finances:

The first step towards financial stability is gaining a clear understanding of your current financial situation. This involves tracking your income, expenses, and debts. There are many budgeting tools and apps available, which can help you analyze your spending patterns and identify areas where you can cut back.

Creating a Budget:

A budget acts as a roadmap for your financial journey, guiding you toward your financial goals. It helps you prioritize spending, allocate funds for essential expenses, and save for the future. A balanced budget ensures that you're living within your means and avoiding unnecessary debt accumulation.

Managing Debt:

Debt can be a significant financial burden for law enforcement officers, particularly student loans, mortgages, and credit card debt. A proactive approach to debt management is essential. Prioritize paying down high-interest debt first, such as credit card debt, to minimize interest charges and reduce your overall debt burden. Consider strategies like debt consolidation or balance transfers to lower interest rates.

Saving for the Future:

It is crucial for officers to plan for their long-term financial security, especially when facing unpredictable career paths and the possibility of unexpected events. This includes establishing an emergency fund to cover unforeseen expenses, such as medical bills or car repairs.

Retirement Planning:

Saving for retirement is paramount for officers, given the often physically demanding nature of their work and the potential for early retirement due to injuries or health concerns. Consider contributing to a 401(k) plan through your employer, taking advantage of any matching contributions offered. Explore other retirement savings options such as a Roth IRA or a traditional IRA.

Understanding Your Benefits:

Take the time to understand the benefits offered by your employer, including health insurance, life insurance, and disability insurance. Make informed decisions regarding your coverage to ensure you have adequate protection in case of unforeseen circumstances.

Practical Tips for Managing Finances:

Set Financial Goals:

Having clear financial goals provides motivation and direction. Set specific, measurable, achievable, relevant, and time-bound (SMART) goals, such as buying a home, paying off debt, or saving for a child's education.

Automate Savings:

Setting up automatic transfers from your checking account to your savings account can help you build a solid savings foundation without relying on willpower alone.

Negotiate Expenses:

Don't hesitate to negotiate expenses, such as your car insurance or utility bills, to potentially save money.

Seek Financial Advice:

If you are feeling overwhelmed by your finances or need assistance with financial planning, consider seeking advice from a qualified financial advisor.

Investing for Your Future:

Investing is a crucial element of long-term financial planning. It allows your money to grow over time, providing the potential for significant returns.

Understanding Your Risk Tolerance:

Before investing, it's essential to understand your risk tolerance. Consider your age, financial situation, and time horizon for investing. If you are young and have a longer investment horizon, you can afford to take on more risk.

Diversification:

Diversification involves spreading your investments across various asset classes, such as stocks, bonds, and real estate, to reduce risk. A diversified portfolio can help mitigate losses if one asset class performs poorly.

Long-Term Perspective:

Investing is a long-term game. Avoid making emotional decisions based on short-term market fluctuations. Focus on your long-term goals and stick to your investment strategy.

Conclusion:

Financial literacy is an essential skill for all law enforcement officers, enabling them to manage their finances effectively and plan for a secure future. By embracing a proactive approach to budgeting, debt management, and saving, officers can achieve financial stability and peace of mind. Furthermore, seeking financial advice from qualified professionals and utilizing available resources can empower officers to make informed financial decisions and navigate their financial journey with confidence. It is imperative that law enforcement agencies prioritize financial literacy training for their officers, recognizing the critical role it plays in supporting their overall well-being and enabling them to serve and protect with greater financial security.

Advocating for Fair Compensation

The financial realities of law enforcement often clash with the noble ideals that draw many to the profession. While officers dedicate their lives to serving and protecting, their paychecks frequently fail to reflect the sacrifices they make. This stark contrast creates a persistent financial struggle, one that can weigh heavily on officers and their families, impacting their well-being and long-term security.

Advocating for fair compensation for law enforcement officers is not merely about seeking a higher paycheck. It's about recognizing the value of their service and ensuring that they are adequately compensated for the risks, responsibilities, and emotional burdens they shoulder. This means fighting for a pay scale that reflects the inherent dangers of the job, the extensive training required, and the 24/7 commitment to public safety.

The fight for fair compensation begins with acknowledging the unique challenges faced by law enforcement. Unlike many professions, policing often involves working irregular hours, including nights, weekends, and holidays, disrupting family life and creating logistical challenges. Officers frequently work overtime, sometimes without additional compensation, further contributing to their financial strain.

Furthermore, the cost of living in many areas, particularly urban centers where crime rates are higher, can make it difficult for officers to make ends meet. The high cost of housing, transportation, and basic necessities can severely impact their financial stability, leading to a constant struggle to balance their budget.

The financial burden extends beyond the cost of living. Law Enforcement officers face significant expenses related to their profession, often borne by them personally. The cost of specialized training, equipment, and personal protective gear can be substantial, adding to their financial stress. Many officers find themselves shouldering the costs of uniforms, firearms, ammunition, and other necessary equipment, expenses that are often not fully covered by their employers.

The issue of debt adds another layer of complexity to the financial challenges faced by officers. Student loans, mortgages, and other financial obligations can weigh heavily on their budgets, making it difficult to save for the future or manage unforeseen expenses. This financial strain can create a cycle of stress and anxiety, impacting their overall well-being and their ability to perform their duties effectively.

To address these challenges, a multifaceted approach is needed.

1. A Comprehensive Review of Pay Scales:

The current pay scales for law enforcement officers must be reviewed and adjusted to reflect the real costs of living, the risks associated with the profession, and the value of their service.

This review should be conducted regularly to ensure that salaries keep pace with inflation and the changing economic landscape.

Addressing pay disparities across different jurisdictions is also crucial, ensuring that officers in high-cost-of-living areas receive compensation that allows them to maintain a decent standard of living.

2. Expanded Benefits Packages:

Officers deserve a comprehensive benefits package that provides financial security and peace of mind. This includes robust health insurance coverage, retirement plans, and access to mental health services.

Expanding these benefits packages would not only improve the quality of life for officers but also attract and retain highly qualified individuals, strengthening the ranks of law enforcement.

3. Addressing the Hidden Costs:

The burden of training, equipment, and personal expenses should be shared more equitably. Employers should contribute significantly to these costs, reducing the financial burden on officers.

Offering affordable training programs, subsidized equipment purchase options, and tax deductions for work-related expenses could alleviate the financial pressure on officers.

4. Promoting Financial Literacy:

Law enforcement agencies should prioritize providing financial literacy education to officers. This includes workshops and programs on budgeting, debt management, investing, and planning for retirement.

Access to financial counseling services could also be provided to officers facing financial difficulties, helping them navigate debt, make informed financial decisions, and secure their financial future.

5. Advocacy and Support:

Law enforcement officers need strong advocacy and support to secure fair compensation and benefits.

This includes working with legislators, unions, and community organizations to raise awareness about the financial challenges faced by officers and advocate for policy changes.

The financial struggles faced by law enforcement officers are not a private matter. They are a systemic problem that affects the entire profession and has a ripple effect on public safety. By acknowledging the unique challenges faced by officers and taking concrete steps to improve their financial well-being, we can ensure that they have the resources and support they need to perform their duties effectively and contribute to safer communities.

The fight for fair compensation is not just about money. It's about valuing the sacrifices made by those who dedicate their lives to protecting us. It's about ensuring that law enforcement officers are not forced to choose between their financial security and their commitment to public service. It's about creating a system that recognizes and rewards their dedication and allows them to live fulfilling lives with the dignity and respect they deserve.

Chapter: 4 The Balancing Act: Juggling Work, Family, and Life

The Shift Work Syndrome

The nature of police work, with its unpredictable hours and demanding schedules, throws a wrench into the gears of a typical family life. Imagine your partner working nights while you're trying to get the kids ready for school. Or picture your spouse rushing off to work just as you're settling in for a quiet evening at home. These scenarios, far from being unusual, are commonplace in law enforcement families. The impact of shift work goes beyond simply missing dinner together; it seeps into every aspect of family dynamics, creating a constant state of adjustment and a longing for normalcy.

The demands of the job often mean missed birthdays, school plays, and family gatherings. Officers might find themselves working holidays, weekends, and even family vacations. It's not just the physical absence that creates a strain; it's the emotional toll. When an officer returns home after a particularly difficult shift, the baggage of their experiences can follow them, impacting their interactions with their loved ones. The line between work and home can blur, creating an invisible burden that weighs heavy on family relationships.

Imagine a police officer, John, who works the night shift. He sees the worst of humanity on a nightly basis. He responds to domestic violence calls, witnesses accidents, and deals with the aftermath of crime. When he finally gets home in the early morning hours, exhausted and emotionally drained, he finds his wife already awake and preparing for work. They have a quick cup of coffee together, but their conversation is strained. John tries to brush off his day, wanting to avoid burdening his wife with the graphic details of his experiences. However, the emotional weight of his work manifests in subtle ways: irritability, anxiety, and difficulty sleeping. His wife notices the changes in his behavior and struggles to understand the underlying causes. The lack of shared experiences and the emotional distance between them create a rift in their relationship.

This scenario, while fictionalized, reflects the reality faced by countless law enforcement families. Shift work not only disrupts the family schedule but also impacts communication, intimacy, and emotional connection. The constant readjustment, the missed moments, and the invisible burden of the job can wear down even the strongest relationships.

The impact of shift work extends to children as well. Imagine a child whose parent works the night shift and is often asleep during the day. This can create a sense of isolation and longing for the presence of a parent. Children might struggle with understanding why their parent is not there for them during the day, leading to feelings of abandonment or resentment. It can also be challenging for children to adjust to their parent's irregular schedule, particularly when it comes to school schedules and extracurricular activities.

Imagine a child, Sarah, whose mother is a police officer. Sarah's mother works the night shift and is often gone when Sarah wakes up in the morning. While Sarah understands that her mother's job is important, she feels lonely and misses having her mother around. Sarah's mother tries to make up for the lost time by spending weekends with her daughter. However, it's not always easy to switch gears from the stress of the job to the joy of family time. Sarah's mother often feels exhausted and withdrawn, making it

difficult for her to fully engage with her daughter. This creates a sense of disconnect between them, leaving Sarah feeling misunderstood and unloved.

These are just a few examples of the many ways that shift work can affect family life. The emotional toll, the missed moments, and the constant adjustments can create a sense of strain and disconnect. However, it's crucial to remember that these challenges are not insurmountable. With open communication, empathy, and a willingness to adapt, law enforcement families can find ways to navigate the demands of the job and nurture strong relationships.

One of the first steps towards navigating the challenges of shift work is to acknowledge its impact on family life. Officers and their families need to be open and honest about the difficulties they face. This means having open conversations about schedules, expectations, and the emotional burden of the job. It also means understanding the invisible weight that officers carry home and offering support without judgment.

For officers, this might involve being mindful of the emotional toll of their work and seeking ways to decompress before coming home. This could include engaging in relaxation techniques, exercising, or spending time in nature. It also means being more communicative with their families about their experiences and seeking support from their partners.

For families, it means understanding the nature of the job and accepting that there will be times when their loved ones are unavailable. It also means finding ways to maintain connection, despite the challenges of irregular schedules. This could involve scheduling regular date nights, celebrating milestones together, and making an effort to spend quality time even when schedules are tight.

The key to navigating these challenges is to build a strong foundation of understanding and support. Families need to work together to create a sense of normalcy amidst the chaos of shift work. They need to prioritize communication, empathy, and finding ways to connect despite the demands of the job. It's not always easy, but with a shared commitment to building a healthy and fulfilling family life, law enforcement families can overcome the obstacles posed by shift work and create a sense of love, stability, and connection.

The Absence of Presence

The impact of missed family milestones and events due to shift work and long hours was a constant source of tension in the lives of many officers. It was a heavy burden, both on the officers themselves and on their families. Imagine the guilt and frustration of missing a child's birthday party or a significant family gathering because you were on a double shift, or even worse, dealing with a major crime scene. The long hours and unpredictable nature of the job often made it impossible to commit to events and activities that were important to family members.

There were stories shared among officers of missed weddings, graduations, and even the birth of children. It was heartbreaking to hear these stories and understand the sense of loss and longing they carried. It wasn't just about missing the events themselves; it was about the sense of distance that grew between the officer and their loved ones. The constant absence could strain relationships and make it difficult for officers to feel fully present and connected to their families.

Sometimes, there was a sense of resignation, a belief that their job demanded this sacrifice, that their family understood and accepted the situation. But that didn't mean it wasn't painful. It was a constant balancing act, a struggle to find a sense of balance between their duty and their desire to be present for the people they loved.

For many officers, this struggle manifested in feelings of guilt. They carried the weight of their absence, the missed moments, and the unspoken feelings. They knew they were missing out on important parts of their families' lives, and it weighed heavily on their hearts.

The officers often felt like they were living in two worlds: the world of law enforcement, where they were dedicated and focused on protecting their community, and the world of family life, where they often felt like an outsider, a ghost in the background. It was a constant tug of war, a struggle to reconcile their duty to their job with their desire to be present and engaged in their families' lives.

Some officers found ways to cope with this challenge. They learned to communicate openly and honestly with their families, explaining the demands of their job and the sacrifices it required. They made an effort to schedule time for family even when their schedules were packed. They found creative ways to stay connected, using technology to stay in touch even when they were away.

But for many, it was a difficult and ongoing struggle. The guilt and the distance were constant reminders of the sacrifices they were making. It was a heavy price to pay for serving their community.

One officer, a veteran of the force, shared his own experience of missing his son's high school graduation because he was working a critical case. He spoke of the deep regret he felt, the sense of isolation he experienced, and the ongoing challenge of bridging that gap with his son. It was a powerful reminder of the human cost of the job, the sacrifice not just of time and energy, but of connection and emotional intimacy.

The stories shared by officers, both in formal interviews and casual conversations, painted a poignant picture of the struggles they faced in balancing their work and their personal lives. They spoke of the loneliness, the guilt, and the fear of being disconnected from their families. These were the unseen costs of the job, the emotional burden that often went unacknowledged.

It wasn't a simple matter of time management or scheduling. It was about a deep-seated sense of duty, a commitment to their job that sometimes felt like it came at the expense of their personal lives.

In the end, the officers knew that their commitment to their work was what defined them, but they also longed for a greater sense of balance, a way to bridge the gap between their two worlds and find a sense of fulfillment in both. It was a challenge they faced every day, and one that highlighted the complexity and the human cost of serving and protecting.

The Invisible Burden

The invisible burden of the job doesn't disappear when the officer clocks out. The stress, trauma, and constant vigilance they experience on duty often seep into their personal lives, casting a long shadow over relationships and overall well-being. It's like carrying a heavy backpack filled with emotional debris, a constant reminder of the darkness they've witnessed and the dangers they've faced. This backpack can weigh them down, impacting their interactions with loved ones, their ability to relax and unwind, and even their physical health.

Imagine a police officer who responds to a horrific car accident, where a family is tragically killed. While they are professionally trained to handle such situations, the emotional toll of witnessing such devastation can be overwhelming. Back home, they might find themselves snapping at their partner for a seemingly insignificant reason, their patience frayed by the day's events. They might struggle to sleep, haunted by the images of the accident, their mind replaying the screams and the carnage. Or perhaps they become withdrawn, finding solace in isolation as they try to process the emotional wreckage.

This invisible burden is not just a psychological issue; it can manifest physically as well. The constant stress can lead to elevated blood pressure, sleep disturbances, digestive issues, and even an increased risk of developing chronic diseases. The body, constantly on high alert, eventually takes a toll, leaving officers feeling drained and depleted.

Relationships, too, are often strained by the demands of the job. The officer's partner may feel neglected, their emotional needs overlooked as the officer grapples with the emotional aftermath of their work. The children may grow up without a fully present parent, their bond with the officer weakened by long hours, missed milestones, and the officer's emotional distance. The officer, caught between the demands of their profession and their personal life, can feel torn, struggling to juggle the weight of their responsibility with the desire to be a loving and attentive partner and parent.

The challenge lies in recognizing this invisible burden and seeking support. Officers often feel pressure to appear strong and stoic, suppressing their emotions and denying the impact of their work. This can lead to a dangerous cycle of isolation and self-denial, preventing them from seeking help and creating a space for healing and emotional recovery.

It's crucial for officers to understand that acknowledging their struggles is not a sign of weakness but a sign of strength. Seeking help from therapists, support groups, or trusted friends and family members can be essential steps towards breaking the cycle of stress and trauma. Open communication with their loved ones, sharing their experiences and the emotional toll they're carrying, can foster understanding and empathy, creating a space for support and connection.

Furthermore, officers need to prioritize self-care, finding healthy ways to manage stress and unwind. This might involve engaging in physical activity, practicing mindfulness techniques, pursuing hobbies, or spending time in nature. These activities can provide a much-needed break from the intensity of their work, allowing them to recharge and reconnect with their own sense of peace and well-being.

The invisible burden of the job is a real and enduring challenge for law enforcement officers. It's a constant reminder that the work they do, while essential for public safety, comes with a heavy price. By acknowledging the impact of their work, seeking support, prioritizing self-care, and fostering open communication with loved ones, officers can begin to manage the invisible burden and maintain a healthier balance between their professional life and personal well-being.

Finding Balance

The constant demands of the job can make it difficult to find a healthy balance between work and personal life. Shift work, long hours, and the inherent stress of the profession often lead to feelings of exhaustion and burnout. However, finding balance is crucial for the well-being of officers and their families.

Time Management Techniques:

Finding balance between work and personal life is an ongoing process, and it requires commitment and effort. By implementing these strategies and utilizing available resources, officers can create a more sustainable and fulfilling life both on and off duty. Remember, taking care of oneself is not a sign of weakness but a sign of strength and resilience.

The Importance of Communication

The importance of open and honest communication between officers and their loved ones cannot be overstated. It is the foundation of a strong and supportive relationship, especially within the demanding context of law enforcement. When officers are able to communicate openly with their spouses, partners, children, or other family members about the challenges they face at work, it creates a space for empathy, understanding, and emotional support. This communication is vital for officers' mental well-being and overall stability.

Imagine a young officer, fresh out of the academy, experiencing his first high-pressure situation. He might have been involved in a tense standoff with a suspect, or witnessed a horrific crime scene. The adrenaline fades, but the emotional impact lingers. His partner might notice a change in his demeanor, a sudden shift in his mood, or a withdrawal from conversations. If this officer has established a foundation of open communication with his family, he can share his experience with his loved ones, talk about the emotions he is feeling, and receive the support he needs.

This communication is not always easy. It often requires officers to confront their own vulnerabilities, to acknowledge the emotional toll of their job, and to let down their guard. But it is in these moments of vulnerability that officers can find the strength to navigate the challenges of their profession.

Family members, in turn, need to understand the unique pressures and demands that officers face. They need to appreciate the emotional toll of the job, the constant exposure to trauma, and the need for a strong support system. An understanding partner might offer a listening ear, a shoulder to cry on, or simply the comforting presence of someone who cares. They might offer practical help, such as taking on more household responsibilities, or simply acknowledging the emotional burden the officer is carrying.

However, the conversation needs to be a two-way street. Officers also need to be understanding and supportive of their loved ones. They need to acknowledge the impact their job has on their family life, the disruptions caused by shift work, and the potential for emotional strain. They need to be willing to listen to their family's concerns, empathize with their experiences, and make an effort to maintain a strong connection even when work demands are high.

The benefits of open communication are immense. It can help to strengthen relationships, reduce stress, improve mental well-being, and create a sense of stability and support for officers. When officers are able to connect with their loved ones, they are better equipped to face the challenges of their job.

Here are some tips for fostering open dialogue with loved ones:

Create a safe space for conversation:

Make time for regular, dedicated conversations with your family, where you can share your experiences, both good and bad, without judgment.

Be honest and transparent:

Don't shy away from difficult conversations about the challenges of the job. Sharing your experiences, even if they are painful, can help your loved ones understand what you are going through.

Be patient and understanding:

Your loved ones may not always understand the realities of your job. It takes time and patience to bridge the gap between your world and theirs.

Seek professional help when needed:

If you or your loved ones are struggling to cope with the emotional toll of the job, don't hesitate to seek professional help from a therapist, counselor, or other mental health professional.

Practice self-care:

Taking care of your mental and physical health is essential for your well-being and your ability to maintain strong relationships.

Find support groups or resources:

There are many support groups and resources available for law enforcement officers and their families.

Open communication is a vital tool for officers to maintain strong relationships and navigate the challenges of their profession. By fostering a culture of honesty, understanding, and support, officers and their loved ones can build strong and resilient bonds that will help them through the toughest times.

Chapter 5: The Blue Wall: The Culture and Camaraderie of Law Enforcement

The Code of Silence

The "code of silence," often referred to as the "blue wall," is a deeply ingrained tradition within law enforcement. This unwritten rule dictates that officers protect one another, even when it means covering up misconduct or wrongdoing. While loyalty and camaraderie are undoubtedly essential elements of any profession, especially one as demanding and dangerous as law enforcement, the code of silence can have profound ethical and societal consequences.

The historical origins of the code of silence can be traced back to the early days of policing when officers faced significant dangers and relied heavily on one another for survival. In a world where law enforcement was often seen as an extension of the powerful elite, officers were often targets of retaliation from those they investigated. This environment fostered a culture of secrecy and mutual protection, where officers learned to trust only their fellow officers.

Over time, this culture of secrecy became ingrained in the fabric of law enforcement, evolving into a complex system of loyalty and discretion. While it may have served a purpose in the past, the code of silence presents significant ethical dilemmas in the modern era.

One of the primary ethical challenges associated with the code of silence is its potential to obstruct justice. When officers are reluctant to report misconduct or wrongdoing committed by their colleagues, it can create a breeding ground for corruption and impunity. This can lead to a culture where officers believe they are above the law and that their actions will not be investigated or punished.

The code of silence also undermines public trust in law enforcement. When officers are perceived as being more concerned with protecting their own than upholding the law, it erodes public confidence in the justice system. This can lead to a cycle of mistrust and hostility between law enforcement and the communities they serve.

The ethical dilemmas surrounding the code of silence are further complicated by the unique pressures faced by law enforcement officers. The constant exposure to violence, trauma, and the threat of danger can create a sense of solidarity and shared experience among officers, making it difficult to turn on one another. Additionally, the fear of retaliation or ostracization can discourage officers from speaking out against wrongdoing.

The legal implications of the code of silence are equally significant. In recent years, there have been numerous cases where officers have been accused of covering up misconduct by their colleagues. These cases have often resulted in legal challenges, investigations, and even criminal charges. While the law prohibits officers from deliberately obstructing justice, the code of silence can create a complex legal landscape where it becomes difficult to prove criminal intent.

To address the ethical and legal challenges posed by the code of silence, significant changes are needed within law enforcement culture. This includes fostering a climate of transparency and accountability where officers are encouraged to report misconduct without fear of retaliation. It also involves implementing robust oversight mechanisms, independent investigations, and strong accountability measures to ensure that officers who break the law are held responsible for their actions.

The path toward dismantling the code of silence is a long and challenging one. It requires a fundamental shift in law enforcement culture, a commitment to ethical conduct, and a willingness to hold officers accountable for their actions. It also requires a renewed focus on building trust and fostering positive relationships between law enforcement and the communities they serve.

The code of silence is a complex and deeply ingrained tradition within law enforcement. While it may have served a purpose in the past, it presents significant ethical and societal challenges in the modern era. By promoting transparency, accountability, and a culture of ethical conduct, we can begin to dismantle the code of silence and create a law enforcement system that is more just, fair, and accountable to the public.

Examples and Case Studies

To illustrate the impact of the code of silence, it is crucial to examine real-world examples and case studies.

The Rodney King Beating

The infamous Rodney King beating, which occurred in 1991, is a stark example of the code of silence in action. Four Los Angeles Police Department officers were caught on video brutally beating King after a high-speed chase. Despite the video evidence, the officers initially claimed they were acting in self-defense. The subsequent trial of the officers revealed a culture of cover-up and a reluctance among officers to speak out against the brutality they witnessed.

The acquittal of the officers in the King beating case sparked widespread protests and riots in Los Angeles, highlighting the deep-seated mistrust between law enforcement and communities of color. It also served as a stark reminder of the dangers of the code of silence and the need for greater transparency and accountability within law enforcement.

The "Blue Wall" in the NYPD

The New York City Police Department (NYPD) has long been known for its strong culture of loyalty and discretion, often referred to as the "blue wall." In recent years, there have been numerous investigations into misconduct and corruption within the NYPD, revealing a pattern of officers covering up for one another and obstructing justice.

One notable example is the case of Daniel Pantaleo, an NYPD officer who was involved in the death of Eric Garner in 2014. Garner died after Pantaleo put him in a chokehold while arresting him for selling loose cigarettes. The chokehold was deemed illegal by the NYPD, and Pantaleo was ultimately fired from the department. However, he was not criminally charged.

Many observers argued that the code of silence played a role in Pantaleo's acquittal, as officers were reluctant to testify against their colleague, even though the evidence of misconduct was clear. The case highlighted the need for reforms within the NYPD to address the pervasive culture of silence and ensure that officers are held accountable for their actions.

The "Blue Code" in Ferguson, Missouri

The events in Ferguson, Missouri, following the fatal shooting of Michael Brown by a police officer in 2014, further exposed the pervasive nature of the code of silence. The investigation into the shooting was marred by conflicting accounts from officers and a lack of transparency from law enforcement.

Many residents of Ferguson alleged that police officers were reluctant to cooperate with investigators, citing the code of silence as a reason for their silence. This lack of transparency fueled public anger and distrust, leading to widespread protests and demonstrations.

The Consequences of the Code of Silence

The consequences of the code of silence are far-reaching and devastating, impacting not only the individuals involved but also the broader community.

Erosion of Public Trust:

The code of silence undermines public trust in law enforcement. When officers are seen as being more concerned with protecting their own than upholding the law, it creates a sense of distrust and resentment between law enforcement and the communities they are sworn to protect. This can lead to a breakdown in communication and cooperation, making it more difficult for police to effectively solve crimes and maintain order.

Perpetuation of Misconduct:

The code of silence can perpetuate misconduct by shielding officers from accountability. When officers know they can count on their colleagues to cover up their mistakes, it can embolden them to engage in illegal or unethical behavior. This can lead to a cycle of abuse, corruption, and impunity within law enforcement agencies.

Obstruction of Justice:

The code of silence can obstruct justice by preventing witnesses from coming forward and evidence from being brought to light. This can make it difficult to prosecute criminals, and it can also lead to wrongful convictions.

Damage to the Profession:

The code of silence can damage the reputation of the entire law enforcement profession. When officers are perceived as being corrupt or untrustworthy, it can make it more difficult for legitimate officers to do their jobs. It can also make it more difficult to recruit and retain qualified officers.

Breaking the Code of Silence

Breaking the code of silence requires a multi-faceted approach that addresses the root causes of the problem and fosters a culture of transparency and accountability.

Transparency and Accountability:

Implementing robust oversight mechanisms, independent investigations, and strong accountability measures is crucial. This means creating a system where officers are encouraged to report misconduct without fear of retaliation and where those who break the law are held accountable for their actions.

Ethical Conduct:

Law enforcement agencies should emphasize ethical conduct and integrity as core values. This means providing officers with comprehensive training on ethical decision-making, cultural sensitivity, and the importance of upholding the law.

Community Engagement:

Building strong relationships with the communities they serve is essential. This means engaging in open dialogue, listening to concerns, and working collaboratively to address community needs.

Support for Whistleblowers:

Providing strong protections and support for officers who come forward to report misconduct is vital. This means creating a safe environment where officers feel empowered to speak up without fear of reprisal.

Conclusion

The code of silence is a dangerous and destructive tradition that has no place in modern law enforcement. Breaking this code requires a commitment to transparency, accountability, and ethical conduct. It also requires a willingness to build trust and foster positive relationships between law enforcement and the communities they serve. By addressing the root causes of the code of silence, we can create a law enforcement system that is more just, fair, and accountable to the public.

The Brotherhood and Sisterhood

The blue wall is more than just a metaphor; it's a tangible reality woven from shared experiences, sacrifices, and a deep sense of brotherhood and sisterhood. It's a bond forged in the crucible of danger, stress, and the constant awareness of the fragility of life. This bond doesn't just exist between sworn officers on a particular force, but extends across departments, agencies, and even nations. It's a sense of kinship that transcends any differences in rank, badge, or uniform.

Imagine a patrol officer, new to the job, responding to a domestic violence call. The adrenaline pumps, the fear of the unknown is palpable, and the weight of responsibility presses down. As they navigate the tense situation, the veteran officer assigned as their partner remains a steady presence, offering guidance, support, and a quiet reassurance that everything will be alright. This experience, and countless others like it, creates a profound sense of camaraderie. The rookie officer, now a seasoned veteran, will carry this shared experience with them throughout their career, knowing they can rely on the support of their fellow officers.

This bond of brotherhood and sisterhood is built on shared experiences, both big and small. The camaraderie of the squad room, the laughter shared during a long shift, the unspoken understanding of the toll the job takes – all contribute to a sense of belonging that is invaluable. Officers understand each other in ways that outsiders simply cannot. They have seen the same horrors, faced the same dangers, and shared the same weight of responsibility. This shared experience fosters a level of trust and empathy that runs deep.

The sacrifices made by law enforcement officers are not always visible. They are often the first responders to tragedies, bearing witness to the worst of humanity. They work long and irregular hours, sacrificing family time and personal well-being for the sake of public safety. They face constant scrutiny and criticism, yet they remain dedicated to their duty. These sacrifices, often made without recognition, strengthen the bonds within the blue wall.

But the blue wall is not without its flaws. The code of silence, a tradition of loyalty and discretion, can sometimes protect misconduct rather than upholding justice. The tendency to prioritize loyalty over accountability can shield officers from scrutiny and prevent necessary reforms. The blue wall can also create a culture of isolation, where officers are reluctant to seek help or admit vulnerability, leading to mental health issues and burnout.

It's crucial to acknowledge that the blue wall, while strong, can be a double-edged sword. While it offers essential support and camaraderie, it can also hinder progress in addressing systemic issues within law enforcement. Recognizing and addressing these challenges is essential for fostering a culture of transparency, accountability, and ethical conduct.

The blue wall can be a force for good, a source of strength and resilience in the face of adversity. But it must be a wall that welcomes change, embraces accountability, and promotes justice for all. This requires a commitment to building a more transparent, inclusive, and ethical culture within law enforcement. It requires a willingness to confront the challenges of the profession, to acknowledge the flaws within the system, and to work tirelessly to create a safer and more just society for everyone.

The story of the blue wall is a complex one, filled with contradictions and paradoxes. It's a story of bravery and sacrifice, but also of vulnerability and the need for reform. It's a story that continues to evolve, shaped by the experiences of the officers who wear the badge and the communities they serve. By understanding the challenges and opportunities presented by the blue wall, we can work together to create a future where law enforcement is a force for good, upholding justice and protecting the rights of all.

The Challenges of Change

The blue wall, a term often used to describe the strong sense of loyalty and camaraderie among law enforcement officers, is a powerful force within the profession. It can be a source of strength and support, but it can also create challenges in promoting change and transparency. The challenge lies in striking a balance between maintaining the bonds of brotherhood and sisterhood and fostering an environment that encourages accountability, reform, and open dialogue.

Addressing systemic issues within the culture of law enforcement is crucial. The "code of silence," a historical tradition of loyalty and discretion, has often been used to protect officers from scrutiny, even when wrongdoing occurs. This can create a climate of impunity where officers feel shielded from accountability, hindering efforts to address corruption and misconduct.

One of the most significant obstacles to change is the perception that speaking out against misconduct or systemic problems within the department can jeopardize one's career or even lead to retribution. This fear of retaliation can deter officers from reporting wrongdoing, perpetuating a culture of silence and hindering progress toward greater transparency and accountability.

Building a culture of transparency requires addressing the root causes of this fear, which include inadequate oversight, a lack of accountability mechanisms, and a lack of trust in internal affairs investigations. Creating independent oversight bodies with the authority to investigate misconduct, ensuring fair and impartial investigations, and protecting whistleblowers from retaliation are crucial steps in fostering a more transparent and accountable system.

Another crucial element in promoting change is addressing issues of bias within law enforcement. Implicit bias, unconscious prejudices that can influence decision-making, can lead to disparities in policing, particularly in communities of color. Recognizing and addressing implicit bias requires ongoing training, awareness campaigns, and a commitment to implementing policies and practices that promote fairness and equality.

Furthermore, fostering an environment of trust and collaboration between law enforcement agencies and the communities they serve is essential for promoting change. Building this trust requires engaging with communities through community policing programs, listening to their concerns, and building relationships based on mutual respect and understanding.

Promoting transparency within the law enforcement culture also involves embracing reform and innovation. This means challenging traditional practices and exploring new approaches to policing that prioritize community engagement, problem-solving, and de-escalation techniques. It also necessitates embracing the use of technology, such as body cameras, to enhance transparency and accountability, while carefully addressing concerns about privacy and potential misuse.

The future of policing depends on a willingness to embrace change and acknowledge the need for reform. This requires strong leadership that promotes ethical practices, encourages open dialogue, and supports efforts to address systemic issues. It also requires a commitment to building trust with the communities served, fostering a culture of accountability, and embracing innovation to meet the evolving challenges of the 21st century. The blue wall, while a powerful symbol of camaraderie, must evolve to become a force for positive change, promoting transparency, accountability, and a more just and equitable system of law enforcement.

The Future of Policing

The future of policing is undeniably intertwined with the need for reform and innovation. The traditional model of law enforcement, rooted in a hierarchical structure and a culture of secrecy, has come under increasing scrutiny in recent years. Calls for greater accountability, transparency, and community engagement have intensified, prompting a critical examination of the "blue wall" and its impact on public trust.

To move forward, law enforcement agencies must embrace a paradigm shift, one that prioritizes community relationships, embraces data-driven strategies, and fosters a culture of transparency and accountability. This requires a multifaceted approach that addresses both the internal culture of law enforcement and the external relationships between police and the communities they serve.

One crucial aspect of reform is the need for a renewed emphasis on **community policing**

. This involves building genuine relationships with residents, engaging in open dialogue, and actively listening to their concerns. Instead of solely responding to crime, community policing emphasizes proactively addressing underlying social issues that contribute to crime, such as poverty, unemployment, and lack of access to resources. By working hand-in-hand with community organizations, schools, and social service agencies, law enforcement can become a more integrated part of the community fabric, fostering trust and building stronger ties.

Transparency is another cornerstone of reform. This involves open and honest communication with the public about police practices, including the use of force, internal investigations, and disciplinary actions. Body cameras, while not a panacea, can play a vital role in enhancing transparency and accountability, providing a more objective record of interactions between officers and the public. Data-driven policing, utilizing crime statistics and other relevant data, can help identify areas with higher crime rates, allocate resources effectively, and inform policing strategies. By making data publicly available, law enforcement agencies can foster greater trust and understanding of their decision-making processes.

Reform also requires addressing systemic issues within law enforcement, including implicit bias, racial profiling, and police brutality. This necessitates comprehensive training programs that focus on de-escalation techniques, cultural competency, and bias awareness. Furthermore, independent oversight bodies, with the power to investigate allegations of misconduct and hold officers accountable, are crucial for ensuring public trust and promoting justice.

Innovative approaches to policing are also essential for the future. This includes exploring new technologies, such as predictive analytics, artificial intelligence, and drone technology, to enhance crime prevention, resource allocation, and public safety. However, the use of such technologies must be carefully scrutinized, ensuring that they are deployed ethically and responsibly, without compromising individual privacy rights.

The future of policing also demands a focus on officer well-being. The demanding nature of the job, coupled with exposure to trauma and stress, can take a heavy toll on officers' mental and physical health. Providing mental health resources, stress management programs, and support networks is crucial for maintaining officer well-being, which in turn, can contribute to better job performance and improved public safety.

Embracing reform and innovation is not simply a matter of adapting to changing times but a moral imperative. It is about ensuring that law enforcement remains a trusted and respected institution, committed to serving the public with integrity, fairness, and a genuine desire to create safer and more just communities. The future of policing hinges on a willingness to confront the challenges of the past, learn from mistakes, and embrace a new vision for law enforcement that reflects the values and aspirations of the 21st century.

The Role of Leadership

Leadership plays an absolutely crucial role in shaping the culture of law enforcement. It's not just about giving orders; it's about setting the tone, embodying the values you want to see in your officers, and creating an environment that fosters trust, accountability, and a commitment to ethical practices. Effective leadership can be the catalyst for positive change, turning a department from a place where questionable tactics are tolerated into a space where integrity and community service are paramount.

Think of it this way: Law enforcement is a profession built on trust. The public trusts that officers will uphold the law fairly, protect their rights, and act with integrity. But that trust is fragile, easily eroded by instances of misconduct or a perception of bias. Good leadership is essential for maintaining that trust, not only with the community but also within the department itself.

Here are some key ways that strong leadership can promote positive change and ethical practices:

1. Setting the Example:

Leaders in law enforcement must lead by example. They need to demonstrate the very values they expect from their officers - integrity, respect, fairness, and compassion. Officers are constantly observing their supervisors, and their behavior serves as a blueprint for how they themselves should conduct themselves. If a leader cuts corners or shows a lack of respect for the law, it sends a message that those behaviors are acceptable. On the other hand, if a leader consistently demonstrates ethical conduct and a commitment to upholding the law, it sends a powerful message that those values are non-negotiable.

2. Creating a Culture of Accountability:

Strong leadership fosters a culture where accountability is not just a word but a reality. This means establishing clear expectations for officer conduct, providing training on ethical decision-making, and having mechanisms in place to investigate allegations of misconduct thoroughly and fairly. It also means creating a climate where officers feel comfortable reporting misconduct without fear of retaliation. This type of culture ensures that bad apples don't spoil the barrel, and it helps to maintain public trust in the department.

3. Embracing Transparency:

Transparency is essential for building trust and legitimacy. Leaders need to be open and honest with the public about their department's actions and decisions. This includes being transparent about investigations, disciplinary actions, and any incidents of misconduct. While there are legitimate concerns about privacy and security, a culture of transparency demonstrates that the department has nothing to hide and that it is committed to accountability.

4. Promoting Community Engagement:

Effective leaders encourage their officers to be active participants in their communities. This means building relationships with community leaders, engaging in community events, and listening to the concerns of residents. Building strong connections with the community can help to bridge the gap between law enforcement and the people they serve. It can also help to identify problems and develop solutions collaboratively.

5. Fostering a Culture of Professionalism:

Leaders play a critical role in creating a culture of professionalism in law enforcement. This means setting high standards for officer conduct, emphasizing the importance of de-escalation, and promoting training in areas such as conflict resolution and cultural sensitivity. It also means encouraging officers to maintain a professional demeanor, even in difficult situations.

6. Prioritizing Officer Well-being:

Strong leadership prioritizes the well-being of their officers. This means providing support for mental health, addressing the challenges of stress and trauma, and fostering a culture where officers feel comfortable seeking help when they need it. It also means addressing issues like burnout and the impact of shift work on personal lives. By taking care of their officers, leaders create a more resilient and effective workforce.

7. Encouraging Innovation and Reform:

Leaders need to be open to new ideas and approaches to policing. This includes embracing innovative technologies, exploring new strategies for community engagement, and addressing systemic issues within the justice system. Leaders must also be willing to acknowledge the need for reform and to work collaboratively with stakeholders to improve the effectiveness and fairness of policing.

8. Leading by Example:

Leaders in law enforcement are not just managers; they are role models. Their actions, their words, and their attitudes have a profound impact on the culture of their department. Every day, they are shaping the way officers view their jobs, their responsibilities, and the community they serve.

Examples of Transformational Leadership:

There are many examples of leaders in law enforcement who have made a real difference in their communities. Here are a few examples:

Chief William Bratton (Los Angeles, New York, Boston):

Bratton is widely credited with leading the transformation of policing in New York City in the 1990s, reducing crime rates and improving community relations. His leadership was characterized by a focus on data-driven strategies, community policing, and accountability.

Chief Michelle Lee (San Francisco):

Lee is a champion of community policing and social justice. She has worked to build bridges between law enforcement and marginalized communities, addressing issues of bias and racial disparities in policing.

Chief Michael Harrison (New Orleans):

Harrison has led the New Orleans Police Department through a period of significant reform following the aftermath of Hurricane Katrina. His leadership has focused on rebuilding trust, promoting transparency, and improving accountability within the department.

The Impact of Leadership:

The impact of leadership on the culture of law enforcement is immeasurable. Leaders set the tone, create the environment, and guide the direction of their departments. They can either perpetuate a culture of secrecy and misconduct or they can foster a culture of trust, accountability, and community service.

The choice is theirs. But the consequences of their decisions reach far beyond the walls of the police station. They impact the safety and well-being of the community, the reputation of law enforcement, and the very fabric of justice.

Chapter 6: The Shadow Side: Facing Corruption and Misconduct

The Abuse of Power

The abuse of power within law enforcement is a dark stain on the otherwise noble profession. It can manifest in various forms, from petty corruption to grand schemes that shake public trust to its core. These instances, unfortunately, are not isolated incidents; they often point to systemic flaws and cultural issues within the system. Here are some examples of cases that expose the ugly side of corruption and misconduct within law enforcement:

1. The Rampant Corruption of the Chicago Police Department:

For decades, the Chicago Police Department has been plagued by allegations of widespread corruption and misconduct. From the notorious "Midnight Crew" scandal in the 1970s to the recent cases of police brutality and excessive force, the city has struggled to address a deep-rooted culture of impunity. One particularly egregious example is the case of the "Hired Truck" scandal, where officers were accused of running a massive scheme involving bribes from towing companies to ensure their vehicles were given preferential treatment. This case, which spanned several years and implicated numerous officers, exposed the systemic corruption that allowed such activities to flourish. The investigation revealed a culture of fear, silence, and cover-up that prevented officers from coming forward with information.

2. The Rogue Unit in Baltimore: The Gun Trace Task Force Scandal:

In Baltimore, a unit known as the Gun Trace Task Force gained notoriety for its involvement in a shocking pattern of robbery, extortion, and drug dealing. The officers, seemingly motivated by greed and a desire to inflate their arrest numbers, planted evidence, framed innocent citizens, and engaged in violent acts of misconduct. Their actions eroded public trust in the police, created a culture of fear in the community, and led to the wrongful imprisonment of innocent individuals. The scandal exposed the dangerous consequences of unchecked power and the need for robust oversight mechanisms to prevent such abuses.

3. The Case of Eric Garner: A Catalyst for Reform:

The death of Eric Garner, a man who was choked to death by a police officer in New York City, sparked nationwide protests and shone a light on the issue of police brutality. Garner was accused of selling loose cigarettes, but the video footage of his arrest, showing him being pinned to the ground and choked for over seven minutes, went viral and sparked widespread outrage. The incident, along with others like the death of Michael Brown in Ferguson, Missouri, and the killing of Freddie Gray in Baltimore, became rallying cries for the Black Lives Matter movement and fueled calls for police reform. While Garner's death did not directly involve corruption in the traditional sense, it highlighted the systemic issues of racial bias, excessive force, and a lack of accountability within the police system.

4. The Ferguson Police Department: A Case of Systemic Bias and Misconduct:

The city of Ferguson, Missouri, became a symbol of racial injustice and police misconduct after the fatal shooting of Michael Brown by a white police officer. The investigation into the shooting, along with a subsequent Department of Justice report, revealed a pattern of systemic bias and misconduct by the Ferguson Police Department. The report found that the department engaged in racial profiling, used excessive force disproportionately against black residents, and generated revenue through fines and fees rather than protecting public safety. The findings led to the resignation of the city's police chief and mayor, as well as a federal oversight agreement aimed at reforming the department's practices.

5. The "Operation Greylord" Investigation: Unveiling Courtroom Corruption:

In the late 1970s and early 1980s, a groundbreaking investigation dubbed "Operation Greylord" exposed a shocking level of corruption within the Cook County, Illinois, court system. Undercover agents infiltrated the system, recording judges taking bribes to influence court decisions. The investigation implicated numerous judges, court officials, and lawyers in a vast conspiracy that undermined the very foundation of justice. This case demonstrated that corruption can infect all levels of the justice system, from the courtroom to the streets. The investigation's impact led to widespread reform efforts within the Cook County court system and served as a stark reminder of the need for vigilance against corruption in all aspects of law enforcement and the justice system.

These examples represent a mere fraction of the cases that have shed light on the dark side of law enforcement. They serve as chilling reminders of the potential for abuse of power and the critical need for transparency, accountability, and reform within the system. The erosion of public trust, the loss of innocent lives, and the damage to the very fabric of society are just some of the devastating consequences of corruption and misconduct.

While these examples focus on high-profile scandals, it's essential to recognize that corruption can manifest in subtler ways, often through everyday practices that go unchecked. These can include:

Abuse of authority:

Officers using their power to intimidate, harass, or discriminate against citizens.

Bias and profiling:

Making decisions based on race, ethnicity, or other factors rather than on objective criteria.

Cover-ups:

Officers protecting one another from accountability for misconduct.

Selective enforcement:

Targeting certain individuals or groups for law enforcement actions while ignoring others.

These subtle forms of corruption can be just as damaging as high-profile scandals, as they undermine public trust and erode the legitimacy of the law enforcement system.

The Root Causes of Corruption:

Understanding the root causes of corruption is crucial for developing effective solutions. Here are some key factors that contribute to the problem:

Systemic Issues:

Inadequate oversight:

Lack of robust oversight mechanisms, such as independent investigations and citizen review boards, can create opportunities for corruption to flourish.

Lack of accountability:

Weak accountability measures, including lenient disciplinary procedures and limited transparency, can encourage officers to act with impunity.

Cultural influences:

A culture of secrecy, loyalty to one's peers, and resistance to outside scrutiny can create an environment where misconduct is tolerated or even encouraged.

Lack of resources:

Insufficient funding, inadequate training, and high workloads can lead to stress, burnout, and a sense of desperation that can contribute to corruption.

Individual Decisions:

Greed and self-interest:

Officers may be motivated by financial gain, such as taking bribes or engaging in illegal activities.

Power and control:

The desire to wield power and influence over others can lead to abuse of authority.

Lack of ethical compass:

A lack of moral principles and a failure to uphold ethical standards can lead to corrupt behavior.

The Consequences of Corruption:

The consequences of corruption within law enforcement are far-reaching and devastating. Here are some of the most significant impacts:

Erosion of Public Trust:

Corruption undermines the public's trust in law enforcement, leading to feelings of fear, resentment, and distrust.

Damage to the Justice System:

Corruption undermines the integrity of the justice system, making it difficult to uphold the rule of law and ensure fair and impartial outcomes.

Increased Crime:

Corruption can lead to a breakdown in law enforcement, creating a climate of lawlessness and fear, which can contribute to an increase in crime.

Erosion of Civic Engagement:

Corruption can discourage citizens from participating in civic affairs and engaging with law enforcement, making it more difficult to address community concerns.

Combating Corruption:

Addressing corruption within law enforcement requires a multi-pronged approach that tackles both systemic and individual factors. Here are some essential strategies:

Robust Oversight Mechanisms:

Implementing strong oversight mechanisms, such as independent investigations, citizen review boards, and body cameras, can provide checks and balances and deter corrupt behavior.

Accountability Measures:

Enacting strong accountability measures, including clear disciplinary guidelines, thorough investigations, and meaningful consequences for misconduct, is crucial.

Transparency and Public Disclosure:

Promoting transparency by making information about law enforcement practices, disciplinary actions, and investigations readily available to the public can help build trust and accountability.

Ethics Training:

Mandating comprehensive ethics training for all law enforcement officers can reinforce ethical principles, promote integrity, and cultivate a culture of accountability.

Community Engagement:

Building strong partnerships with community members and fostering open communication can help identify and address issues of corruption and misconduct.

Upholding Ethical Conduct:

The fundamental principle underlying law enforcement is the unwavering commitment to uphold the law, protect citizens, and serve the public interest. Ethical conduct is not just a matter of following rules; it's about embodying core values, such as honesty, integrity, fairness, and respect. Officers must understand that their actions have a profound impact on individuals, communities, and the fabric of society. They must strive to uphold the law, treat all individuals with dignity and respect, and remain vigilant against the temptations of corruption and misconduct.

By confronting the shadow side of law enforcement, acknowledging the root causes of corruption, and implementing effective strategies for prevention and accountability, we can work toward a future where law enforcement serves as a true force for justice and protection, earning the trust and respect of the communities it serves.

The Root Causes of Corruption

The existence of corruption within law enforcement is a complex and multifaceted issue, with roots that intertwine systemic factors and individual choices. It's a dark undercurrent that can undermine the very foundation of justice and public trust. Understanding the root causes is crucial to developing effective strategies for combating this insidious force.

Systemic factors play a significant role in creating fertile ground for corruption to flourish. Inadequate oversight and accountability mechanisms can create a sense of impunity, allowing misconduct to thrive unchecked. When there are limited independent investigations, weak disciplinary procedures, and a lack of transparency in internal affairs, it becomes easier for officers to engage in unethical or illegal activities without fear of serious consequences. This breeds a culture of cynicism, where the focus shifts from serving the public to protecting oneself and one's colleagues, even at the expense of justice.

The influence of cultural norms within law enforcement can also contribute to a climate where corruption is more likely to take root. The "blue wall of silence," a code of loyalty and discretion among officers, can discourage whistleblowing and create an environment where wrongdoing is protected. This "us against them" mentality can make it difficult for officers to challenge unethical behavior, even when they witness it.

Furthermore, the pressure to maintain a tough image, combined with a lack of comprehensive training on ethics and de-escalation techniques, can lead to officers resorting to excessive force or engaging in discriminatory practices. The lack of diversity within law enforcement agencies can exacerbate this issue, creating a culture that is less responsive to the needs of diverse communities and more susceptible to biases and prejudice.

Individual decisions, driven by greed, power, or a sense of entitlement, also play a crucial role in fostering corruption. Officers who view their position as a means to gain personal advantage, rather than a public service, are more likely to engage in bribery, extortion, or other forms of misconduct. The allure of power can lead individuals to abuse their authority, prioritizing their own interests over the well-being of the community they are sworn to protect.

The desire for personal enrichment can also be a potent motivator for corruption. When salaries are low, opportunities for overtime are limited, or promotions are scarce, some officers may resort to illegal activities to supplement their income. This can create a cycle of dependence on corrupt practices, where officers become trapped in a system they feel they cannot escape.

The consequences of corruption within law enforcement are far-reaching and devastating. It erodes public trust in the justice system, undermines the rule of law, and perpetuates inequality and injustice. When citizens lose faith in the police, they are less likely to report crimes, cooperate with investigations, or respect the law. This can lead to a decline in public safety, as criminals feel emboldened by the perception that they can operate with impunity.

Moreover, corruption within law enforcement can have a profound impact on the lives of individuals. Victims of abuse of power, discrimination, or wrongful convictions can experience lasting trauma, loss of faith in the system, and a sense of powerlessness. It is essential to acknowledge the human cost of corruption and the lasting damage it can inflict on communities and individuals.

Combating corruption requires a multi-pronged approach that addresses both systemic and individual factors. Robust oversight mechanisms, such as independent investigations, civilian review boards, and rigorous internal affairs units, are essential to deterring misconduct and holding officers accountable for their actions.

Strengthening accountability measures, including transparent disciplinary procedures, public reporting of misconduct cases, and the swift removal of officers who engage in corrupt activities, are crucial to restoring public trust.

Investing in comprehensive training programs that emphasize ethics, de-escalation techniques, diversity and inclusion, and conflict resolution can help to shape a more ethical and accountable culture within law enforcement.

Furthermore, promoting positive leadership that emphasizes integrity, accountability, and community engagement is vital to fostering a culture that values ethical conduct and public service.

Combating corruption within law enforcement is not simply a matter of enforcing rules or punishing wrongdoers. It is about creating a system that prioritizes ethics, accountability, and public service. This requires a collective commitment from law enforcement agencies, policymakers, and the public to create a culture that values integrity and upholds the principles of justice.

The Consequences of Corruption

The erosion of trust is perhaps the most devastating consequence of corruption. When people lose faith in the very institutions designed to protect them, it undermines the entire foundation of law and order. Public trust is essential for the effective functioning of any law enforcement agency. When corruption becomes prevalent, it breeds cynicism and distrust, making it difficult for officers to gain the cooperation and support of the community they are supposed to serve. This lack of trust can lead to a reluctance to report crimes, a refusal to cooperate with investigations, and a general sense of alienation between the police and the public.

A prime example of the devastating impact of corruption on public trust can be found in the infamous Watergate scandal. The Watergate scandal, a political scandal that began in 1972, exposed a web of illegal activities within the Nixon administration, including break-ins, wiretapping, and cover-ups. The subsequent investigation and public hearings revealed a deep culture of corruption and abuse of power within the highest levels of government. The revelations shattered public trust in the government, leading to a decline in civic engagement and a sense of disillusionment with the political system.

Moreover, corruption undermines the integrity of the justice system, leading to a sense of injustice and unfairness. When officers engage in corrupt practices such as bribery, extortion, or planting evidence, it undermines the very principles of justice and fairness that the system is supposed to uphold. This can lead to wrongful convictions, the dismissal of legitimate cases, and a sense of impunity for criminals. The consequences of such injustices can be far-reaching, damaging innocent lives and creating a climate of fear and uncertainty.

The erosion of trust and the integrity of the justice system have a direct and tangible impact on public safety. When people lose faith in law enforcement, they are less likely to report crimes, making it more difficult for police to investigate and solve cases. This can lead to an increase in crime, as criminals feel emboldened by the perceived weakness of the law. Furthermore, corruption within law enforcement can create a breeding ground for organized crime, as criminals may seek to exploit corrupt officers for their own benefit.

The impact of corruption on public safety is particularly profound in communities that have already experienced systemic marginalization and discrimination. When law enforcement agencies are perceived as corrupt or biased, it can further erode trust and create a sense of hopelessness within these communities. This can lead to a cycle of distrust and alienation, making it difficult for officers to build positive relationships with the people they are supposed to protect.

In conclusion, corruption within law enforcement has a profound and devastating impact on public trust, the integrity of the justice system, and overall public safety. It breeds cynicism, distrust, and a sense of injustice, creating a climate of fear and uncertainty. To effectively address corruption, it is essential to implement robust oversight mechanisms, promote transparency and accountability, and cultivate a culture of ethical conduct within law enforcement. By prioritizing integrity, transparency, and accountability, we can work towards restoring public trust and ensuring that law enforcement agencies truly serve and protect all members of society.

Combating Corruption

Combating corruption within law enforcement is not just a matter of catching bad apples; it's about addressing systemic issues that create fertile ground for misconduct. Oversight and accountability are the cornerstones of preventing corruption and restoring public trust. It's about establishing mechanisms that ensure transparency, deter unethical behavior, and provide avenues for justice when transgressions occur.

Robust oversight mechanisms are critical. These involve independent bodies with the authority to investigate allegations of corruption without fear or favor. These bodies should have the resources, expertise, and legal framework to conduct thorough investigations and hold accountable those who abuse their power. Transparency is essential. Public access to information about investigations, disciplinary actions, and internal policies helps to ensure public confidence in the system and deter misconduct.

Independent investigations are crucial for upholding the integrity of the justice system. When allegations arise, they need to be investigated by agencies free from any influence or pressure from the law enforcement agency involved. This independence ensures objectivity and impartiality, crucial for uncovering the truth and holding those responsible to account.

Strong accountability measures are vital to deter corruption. This includes clear guidelines, policies, and codes of conduct outlining expected behavior and the consequences for violations. Disciplinary actions must be fair, consistent, and proportionate to the severity of the misconduct. This includes both internal disciplinary processes and external accountability measures, such as criminal prosecution for serious offenses.

Public involvement is a critical component of combating corruption. Citizen oversight groups, community forums, and open communication channels provide platforms for public input, concerns, and complaints. This engagement helps to identify potential areas for improvement and promote transparency in the system.

However, combating corruption is not merely about imposing regulations. It's about fostering a culture of ethics and integrity within law enforcement. This involves training officers about ethical decision-making, promoting a strong sense of public service, and encouraging officers to report wrongdoing without fear of retaliation. Building a culture of accountability requires a collective effort from every level of the law enforcement system, including leadership, supervisors, and individual officers.

The fight against corruption is an ongoing battle that requires constant vigilance. By implementing robust oversight mechanisms, conducting independent investigations, imposing strong accountability measures, and fostering a culture of ethical conduct, we can effectively combat corruption and restore public trust in law enforcement.

Here are some real-world examples that illustrate the importance of these strategies:

The New York City Civilian Complaint Review Board (CCRB):

The CCRB is an independent agency that investigates complaints of police misconduct in New York City. Its independence allows it to investigate allegations without interference from the NYPD, fostering greater public confidence in the process.

The Independent Police Oversight Commission (IPOC) in Los Angeles:

The IPOC is a civilian oversight body that has the authority to investigate allegations of police misconduct, recommend disciplinary action, and make policy recommendations. The IPOC's existence has been credited with increasing transparency and accountability within the LAPD.

The Justice Department's Civil Rights Division:

This division investigates allegations of civil rights violations by law enforcement agencies across the country. Its investigations often lead to significant reforms and policy changes, holding police departments accountable for their actions.

The Whistleblower Protection Act:

This federal law protects employees who report wrongdoing within their agencies. By encouraging whistleblowers to come forward, the act helps to uncover corruption and ensure that misconduct is addressed.

These examples demonstrate the impact that robust oversight and accountability mechanisms can have on combating corruption in law enforcement. They highlight the importance of independent investigations, clear disciplinary processes, and public involvement in holding law enforcement accountable for its actions.

In conclusion, combating corruption in law enforcement requires a multifaceted approach that addresses both systemic issues and individual misconduct. Robust oversight mechanisms, independent investigations, strong accountability measures, and a culture of ethics are essential components of preventing corruption and restoring public trust. By implementing these strategies, we can work towards a more just and equitable system of law enforcement.

The Importance of Ethical Conduct

Ethical conduct is the bedrock of law enforcement. It's not just a set of rules or guidelines; it's the very soul of the profession. The oath sworn by every officer is a solemn promise to uphold the law, protect citizens, and serve the public interest. This commitment to ethical behavior is paramount, shaping the way officers interact with the community, respond to situations, and make decisions that impact lives.

The weight of upholding the law rests heavily on an officer's shoulders. It's a responsibility that demands unwavering integrity and adherence to the principles of justice. Every action taken, every word spoken, and every decision made must be guided by the law, ensuring fairness and impartiality. This requires constant vigilance, a keen awareness of ethical boundaries, and a steadfast commitment to upholding the law, even in the face of pressure or temptation.

Protecting citizens is the core mission of law enforcement. It's a duty that transcends the pursuit of justice, demanding compassion, empathy, and a genuine concern for the well-being of those entrusted to their care. This means treating all individuals with dignity and respect, regardless of their background, beliefs, or circumstances. It also requires officers to act with restraint and judgment, employing de-escalation techniques when possible and using force only as a last resort.

Serving the public interest is not simply a job; it's a calling. It requires a commitment to the greater good, putting the needs of the community above personal gain or agendas. This involves building trust with the community, engaging in open and honest dialogue, and working collaboratively to address issues of concern. It also means holding oneself accountable for actions, striving for transparency and responsiveness, and being willing to admit mistakes and learn from them.

The ethical compass guides officers through challenging situations and difficult choices. It helps them navigate the gray areas of the law, make sound judgment calls, and uphold the integrity of the profession, even when faced with pressure or temptation. Ethical conduct is not just a matter of personal choice; it's a fundamental requirement for maintaining public trust, ensuring the effectiveness of law enforcement, and upholding the principles of justice.

The importance of ethical conduct is underscored by the devastating consequences of its absence. Corruption and misconduct erode public trust, undermine the rule of law, and create a climate of fear and distrust. When officers abuse their power, engage in illegal activities, or fail to uphold the law, they betray the public's trust, damage the reputation of the profession, and ultimately hinder their ability to serve and protect.

Ethical conduct is not merely an abstract concept; it's a practical necessity for effective law enforcement. It fosters a positive relationship between officers and the community, enabling them to work collaboratively to prevent crime, solve problems, and create safer and more just environments.

Every officer, at every level, has a responsibility to uphold ethical standards. This includes being honest, respectful, fair, and accountable in their actions and decisions. It also means refusing to participate in any form of corruption or misconduct, and reporting any unethical behavior they witness.

The pursuit of justice is a noble calling, demanding unwavering integrity and commitment to ethical principles. By upholding these standards, law enforcement officers can build trust, promote safety, and contribute to a more just and equitable society. It's a responsibility that requires constant vigilance, a keen awareness of ethical boundaries, and a steadfast commitment to serving the public interest.

Chapter 7: The Battle for Justice: Dealing with Difficult Cases and Ethical Dilemmas

The Gray Areas of Law

The gray areas of law are a constant challenge for law enforcement officers. They often find themselves navigating complex situations where the letter of the law is unclear or conflicting, requiring them to make difficult decisions that carry significant weight. This can lead to ethical dilemmas that challenge their principles and judgment.

Imagine a scenario where an officer witnesses a group of teenagers vandalizing public property. They know that vandalism is a crime, but they also recognize that these are young individuals who may be making a mistake. Should they immediately arrest them, potentially impacting their future, or take a more lenient approach, attempting to teach them a lesson instead?

The answer is not always clear-cut, and officers must weigh several factors in making their decision. The severity of the vandalism, the age and background of the individuals involved, the potential consequences of their actions, and the officer's own personal values all come into play.

Another example involves a case where an officer suspects an individual of drug possession but lacks concrete evidence. They may have observed suspicious behavior, but not enough to justify a search or arrest. Should they press forward with a search, potentially violating the individual's rights, or let them go, risking the possibility that they are dealing drugs?

This dilemma reflects a crucial tension between upholding the law and respecting individual rights. Officers must be careful not to infringe on constitutional protections while also ensuring that their actions are effective in deterring criminal activity.

In cases involving domestic violence, officers may face even more complex situations. They may arrive at a scene where the victim is reluctant to press charges, potentially fearing retaliation from their abuser. Should the officer push for charges, risking the victim's safety, or respect their wishes, even if it means potentially allowing the abuse to continue?

These scenarios highlights the delicate balancing act that officers must perform, weighing the needs of victims against the rights of the accused. Their decisions have far-reaching consequences, and they often face criticism from both sides.

The ethical dilemmas officers face are not always easy to resolve. There are no simple answers or clear-cut solutions. It is important to remember that the gray areas of law often reflect the complexities of human behavior, and officers must use their judgment, training, and empathy to make decisions that uphold justice and protect both the public and individual rights.

One of the most challenging aspects of dealing with these gray areas is the constant pressure to "make the right call." Officers are often expected to make decisions with limited information and under immense pressure. The weight of their decisions can be significant, especially when they may have to deal with the consequences of their actions, even if they acted in good faith.

It is crucial for law enforcement agencies to provide their officers with the training and support they need to navigate these complex situations. This includes training in ethics, de-escalation techniques, and understanding the nuances of the law. Agencies should also establish clear guidelines and protocols to help officers make informed decisions in difficult circumstances.

Beyond training, officers need access to resources and support systems to help them manage the stress and emotional toll of dealing with these challenging situations. This includes access to mental health professionals, peer support groups, and confidential reporting systems.

Recognizing the emotional and psychological burdens that officers face, and providing them with the resources to cope, is crucial for ensuring their well-being and their ability to make sound judgment calls in difficult situations.

The gray areas of law are not just an intellectual challenge for officers; they are also an emotional one. They are constantly wrestling with the tension between upholding the law and respecting individual rights, and their decisions can have a profound impact on the lives of those involved.

By acknowledging the complexity of these situations, providing officers with the training, support, and resources they need, and fostering a culture of ethical decision-making, we can help law enforcement officers navigate the gray areas of law with greater clarity and compassion.

The Burden of Proof

The courtroom is a battleground. It's a place where the pursuit of justice collides with the protection of individual rights. On one side, you have the victims, yearning for accountability and a sense of closure. On the other, you have the accused, shielded by the Constitution's promise of due process. Balancing these two forces is the delicate art of the legal system, and it's a balancing act that often leaves everyone feeling frustrated.

This subsection delves into the critical interplay between seeking justice for victims and respecting the rights of the accused. It explores the concept of due process, a fundamental principle of the American legal system, and its vital role in ensuring fairness and protecting individuals from arbitrary government actions.

Due process is not a mere formality; it's the bedrock of our legal system. It ensures that every individual, regardless of their social status, background, or the nature of the accusations against them, receives a fair hearing before the law. The principle is enshrined in the Fifth and Fourteenth Amendments to the Constitution, guaranteeing both procedural and substantive due process. Procedural due process focuses on the fairness of the procedures used by the government in making decisions that affect individuals.

This includes everything from the right to notice and an opportunity to be heard, to the right to counsel and the right to confront one's accusers. Substantive due process, on the other hand, addresses the fairness of the law itself. It ensures that laws are not arbitrary or capricious, and that they serve a legitimate governmental interest.

These safeguards are crucial in preventing the abuse of power and ensuring that innocent people are not unjustly punished. However, these protections can also complicate the pursuit of justice, especially in cases where the evidence is overwhelming and the crime is particularly heinous. It's easy to feel frustrated by the system's seeming unwillingness to deliver swift retribution, but understanding the rationale behind due process is essential.

For those who have lost loved ones to crime, the legal process can feel slow and emotionally taxing. They want to see justice served, and they want to see the person responsible held accountable. But the justice system is not designed to deliver immediate gratification. It's designed to be fair and impartial, ensuring that everyone has a chance to be heard, regardless of their guilt or innocence.

This commitment to fairness means that the prosecution bears the burden of proof, and the accused is presumed innocent until proven guilty. This presumption of innocence is not a technicality; it's a fundamental principle that protects individuals from being convicted based on suspicion or prejudice. The prosecution must present compelling evidence, beyond a reasonable doubt, to convince a jury or judge of the accused's guilt. This standard of proof is high, and it is designed to prevent wrongful convictions.

The burden of proof is an essential safeguard, ensuring that innocent people are not punished for crimes they did not commit. But it can also be a source of frustration for victims and their families. They may feel that the system is not adequately protecting their interests, and they may feel that the focus is more on protecting the rights of the accused than on seeking justice for them.

Navigating this complex landscape is a constant challenge for law enforcement officers. They are tasked with upholding the law, protecting the public, and ensuring that criminals are brought to justice. However, they must also respect the rights of the accused and ensure that they receive a fair trial.

This often means walking a tightrope. They must be both compassionate and objective, understanding the pain of victims while also ensuring that the rights of the accused are not violated. This is a delicate dance, and one that requires both skill and sensitivity.

There have been instances where the weight of evidence seems undeniable, yet due process mandates that the accused still receives a fair trial. The case of O.J. Simpson stands out as a prime example of this. The evidence against him was strong, including DNA evidence linking him to the crime scene, but the jury ultimately acquitted him. This outcome, while controversial, highlights the importance of due process and the presumption of innocence, even in high-profile and emotionally charged cases.

The O.J. Simpson trial also serves as a reminder that the legal system is not perfect. It can be slow, cumbersome, and even frustrating at times. But it's the best system we have for ensuring fairness and protecting individual rights.

The legal system is designed to provide both due process for the accused and justice for the victims. However, achieving this balance is not always easy. It requires a nuanced understanding of the law, a commitment to fairness, and a willingness to engage in difficult conversations about the limits of justice.

It is crucial to remember that every case is unique, and each individual deserves a fair hearing. The pursuit of justice is a complex and nuanced process, and it often requires compromises and difficult decisions. The responsibility of upholding the law, protecting the public, and ensuring that justice is served lies on the shoulders of law enforcement officers. It's a responsibility they carry with honor, dedication, and a commitment to upholding the principles of a fair and just society.

The Search for Truth

The search for truth is at the heart of every investigation. It's a quest for answers, a pursuit of justice, and a commitment to fairness. But it's not a simple task. It's a complex and demanding process that requires unwavering dedication, a keen eye for detail, and an unyielding commitment to objectivity.

Law enforcement officers face the challenge of sifting through a maze of information, piecing together fragments of evidence, and navigating the often-foggy terrain of human perception. They must carefully consider every piece of the puzzle, recognizing that even the smallest detail can hold the key to unlocking a case.

The investigative process is a dance between meticulous observation and critical thinking. It's about understanding the nuances of human behavior, the intricacies of crime scenes, and the delicate balance between gathering evidence and preserving the integrity of the investigation. Each step requires a delicate touch, a careful balance between assertiveness and restraint, and a deep respect for the law and the rights of all involved.

Every case presents its own set of obstacles. Some investigations unfold like meticulously crafted narratives, with clear timelines and readily available evidence. But more often, the truth is shrouded in ambiguity, obscured by conflicting accounts, and hidden in the shadows of human deception.

The detectives must navigate through a labyrinth of contradictions, inconsistencies, and deliberate obfuscation. They must separate fact from fiction, separating genuine leads from deliberate misdirection. Their success hinges on their ability to decipher the complexities of human motivations, the art of deception, and the subtle clues that betray the truth.

Gathering evidence is often a delicate and intricate process. It's a meticulous search for tangible proof, a quest for the physical remnants of a crime, and a careful documentation of every detail. It requires a keen eye for observation, a strong understanding of forensic science, and the ability to identify and collect evidence without compromising the integrity of the crime scene.

But the search for truth is not solely about finding physical evidence. It's also about piecing together the narrative of a case, understanding the context, and considering the human factors involved. It's about delving into the motivations of the perpetrators, the vulnerabilities of the victims, and the web of relationships that intertwine around the crime.

It's about interviewing witnesses, carefully listening to their accounts, and discerning the truth from the distortions of memory, self-preservation, and bias. It's about piecing together a puzzle, recognizing the patterns, and revealing the unseen connections.

This is where the art of investigation truly comes into play. It's about the ability to see beyond the surface, to understand the unspoken, and to interpret the nuances of human behavior. It's about recognizing the subtle cues, the nervous twitches, the evasive answers, and the fleeting expressions that betray a hidden truth.

The most challenging cases are often those where the truth is elusive, shrouded in mystery, and veiled by the intentions of those involved. These are the investigations that push detectives to the limits of their abilities, forcing them to confront the shadows of human nature and the intricacies of human deception.

These are the cases that require unwavering determination, a relentless pursuit of the truth, and a deep understanding of the human psyche. It's a journey into the darkness, a search for answers in the midst of uncertainty, and a commitment to justice, even when the path is fraught with challenges.

But even with the best intentions and the most skilled investigators, the search for truth is never guaranteed. The world is a complex and unpredictable place, and human behavior is often shrouded in ambiguity. The truth may be elusive, it may be incomplete, or it may never be fully revealed.

But for those dedicated to seeking justice, the pursuit of the truth is a mission, a calling, and a never-ending quest. It's a commitment to fairness, a dedication to accountability, and a belief in the power of evidence to bring light to the darkness.

Every case is a unique puzzle, a story waiting to be told, and a search for answers that can only be achieved through meticulous investigation, unwavering determination, and an unyielding commitment to seeking the truth.

The Impact Bias

Implicit bias, a form of unconscious prejudice, has infiltrated various aspects of society, including law enforcement. It's a pervasive issue that can manifest in subtle ways, influencing officers' perceptions, decisions, and actions without their conscious awareness. Recognizing and addressing implicit bias is paramount for promoting fairness and impartiality within law enforcement.

Imagine a patrol officer responding to a domestic violence call. The officer, perhaps unconsciously influenced by implicit bias, might perceive a person of color as more likely to be the aggressor than a white individual in a similar situation. This bias, rooted in societal stereotypes and ingrained patterns of thinking, can lead to unfair treatment, escalation of the situation, and potentially even a wrongful arrest.

Implicit bias doesn't discriminate based on race alone. It can manifest in relation to gender, sexual orientation, socioeconomic status, and other social categories. An officer might unconsciously associate young men with criminality or view women as less capable of committing violent crimes, skewing their perception of a situation. This bias can manifest in various ways, such as:

Disproportionate use of force:

Studies have shown that people of color are more likely to be subjected to excessive force by law enforcement officers, even when controlling for other factors like crime rates. This can be attributed, in part, to implicit bias influencing officers' perceptions of threat.

Premature judgments:

Implicit bias can lead to premature judgments about individuals based on their appearance, demeanor, or other superficial factors. This can result in unfair profiling, discriminatory treatment, and inaccurate assessments of individuals' behavior.

Unconscious stereotyping:

Implicit bias can reinforce unconscious stereotypes about certain groups, leading officers to make assumptions about individuals based on their race, ethnicity, or other social categories. This can affect how officers interact with individuals, potentially leading to unfair treatment and biased decision-making.

The consequences of implicit bias in law enforcement are far-reaching and detrimental. It can erode public trust, undermine the legitimacy of the justice system, and contribute to racial disparities in policing. It can also lead to wrongful convictions, excessive use of force, and the escalation of conflicts that could have been resolved peacefully.

Recognizing the presence of implicit bias is the first step towards addressing it. Law enforcement agencies and individual officers need to be aware of the potential for unconscious bias to influence their decisions and actions. This can be achieved through:

Training and education:

Implementing mandatory training programs that educate officers about implicit bias, its effects, and strategies for mitigating its impact. These programs should use interactive exercises, real-life scenarios, and case studies to help officers develop a deeper understanding of the issue.

Data collection and analysis:

Collecting and analyzing data on police encounters to identify patterns of bias and disproportionate outcomes. This information can help agencies identify areas where implicit bias may be affecting their operations and implement targeted interventions.

Community engagement:

Engaging with community members, including those from marginalized groups, to gain insights into their experiences with law enforcement and address concerns about bias and discrimination. This can help bridge the gap between law enforcement and the communities they serve, building trust and fostering positive relationships.

Accountability and oversight:

Establishing robust systems of accountability and oversight to monitor and address instances of bias and misconduct within law enforcement. This can include independent reviews, body cameras, and citizen complaint procedures.

Addressing implicit bias requires a multifaceted approach, involving individual officers, law enforcement agencies, and the broader community. It's not about blaming individuals but rather about creating a system that promotes fairness, impartiality, and respect for all members of society.

Beyond training and awareness, there are specific strategies officers can employ to mitigate the influence of implicit bias in their decision-making:

Slowing down:

Taking a moment to pause and consider the potential for bias before making a decision. This can help officers become more aware of their unconscious biases and make more deliberate choices.

Seeking diverse perspectives:

Actively seeking out perspectives from diverse colleagues and community members to challenge their own assumptions and biases. This can help officers develop a more nuanced understanding of complex situations.

Using objective criteria:

Focusing on objective criteria, such as evidence, witness statements, and relevant policies, rather than relying on intuition or stereotypes when making decisions. This helps to reduce the influence of unconscious biases.

Practicing empathy and compassion:

Making an effort to understand the perspectives and experiences of those they interact with, fostering empathy and compassion, can help officers to see individuals as human beings rather than stereotypes.

The battle against implicit bias in law enforcement is an ongoing one. It requires a commitment to ongoing education, training, and self-reflection, as well as a willingness to challenge societal norms and prejudices. By embracing these strategies, law enforcement agencies and individual officers can work towards creating a more just and equitable system, where all individuals are treated fairly and with respect, regardless of their race, ethnicity, gender, or other social categories.

The Pursuit of Justice

The pursuit of justice is not simply a theoretical concept but a tangible reality woven into the fabric of every interaction law enforcement officers have with the community. It is a guiding principle that drives their actions, shaping their decisions and informing their responses to the complexities of crime and human suffering. This commitment to justice manifests in a profound dedication to protecting the vulnerable, seeking fair outcomes for victims, and upholding the principles of fairness and equality that form the bedrock of a just society.

Imagine the scene: a domestic violence call. The officer arrives, heart pounding, not knowing what to expect. The air crackles with tension, the weight of fear hanging heavy in the room. This is the face of vulnerability, of human beings stripped bare by violence and fear. The officer, armed with training and empathy, navigates this delicate situation, first and foremost ensuring the safety of the victim. This is the essence of their commitment—to be a shield against harm, a voice for the voiceless, and a symbol of hope in a moment of despair.

Protecting the vulnerable extends beyond physical harm. It encompasses the emotional well-being of those who have suffered trauma, the victims of crime who are left reeling in the aftermath of violence. It is the compassionate ear that listens without judgment, the hand extended to help navigate a complex legal system, the voice that speaks truth to power on behalf of those who feel powerless. This pursuit of justice is not solely about punishment; it is about healing, about empowering victims to reclaim their lives and rebuild their sense of safety and security.

Seeking fair outcomes for victims is not just a matter of ensuring that perpetrators are held accountable. It is about ensuring that victims are treated with dignity and respect throughout the legal process, their voices heard and their needs met. It is about providing support and resources to help them heal, cope, and rebuild their lives. This commitment to fairness demands that law enforcement officers remain vigilant against bias, ensuring that the scales of justice are balanced and that every individual, regardless of background or circumstance, is treated with equal consideration and fairness.

The pursuit of justice requires a constant striving for fairness, a relentless pursuit of truth, and an unwavering commitment to upholding the principles that form the foundation of a just society. It is a journey paved with challenges, fueled by compassion, and driven by an unwavering belief in the inherent worth of every human being. It is in the faces of those who have found solace in the presence of law enforcement, in the stories of those who have seen justice prevail, that the true measure of this pursuit is found. It is a testament to the power of human courage, resilience, and unwavering commitment to safeguarding the vulnerable and seeking fair outcomes for all.

Chapter 8: The Changing Landscape: The Role of Technology and innovation in Law Enforcement

The Digital Age of Policing

The integration of technology into law enforcement has brought about a seismic shift in how policing operates, transforming the way officers gather intelligence, respond to incidents, and interact with the public. From the ubiquitous body cameras that have become a symbol of transparency and accountability to the sophisticated data analysis tools that offer predictive capabilities, technology has become an indispensable tool for modern law enforcement.

The Rise of Body Cameras

The proliferation of body cameras has fundamentally altered the landscape of policing. Initially met with some resistance, body cameras have proven to be a powerful tool for increasing transparency, accountability, and public trust. They provide objective evidence in cases of alleged police misconduct, ensuring that both officers and the public are held accountable for their actions. Body camera footage has been instrumental in resolving disputes, exonerating officers from false accusations, and providing crucial evidence in criminal investigations. Beyond their role in accountability, body cameras also contribute to de-escalation tactics, as officers are more conscious of their actions knowing that they are being recorded.

Surveillance Systems: The Evolving Landscape

Surveillance systems, ranging from CCTV cameras to facial recognition technology, have become increasingly prevalent in urban environments and public spaces. While these systems offer valuable benefits in crime prevention, apprehension, and investigation, they also raise significant concerns about privacy and civil liberties. The use of facial recognition technology, for instance, has generated heated debates about its potential for misuse, especially in situations where individuals are unknowingly identified and tracked. Balancing the potential benefits of surveillance with the need to protect individual privacy rights remains a complex and ongoing challenge for policymakers and law enforcement agencies.

Data Analysis and Predictive Policing

The advent of Big Data and advanced analytics has ushered in a new era of predictive policing. Law enforcement agencies are now leveraging sophisticated algorithms to analyze large datasets, identify patterns, and predict potential crime hotspots. This information can inform resource allocation, targeted patrol strategies, and proactive interventions. However, the use of predictive policing raises concerns about potential biases in the algorithms used, as well as the ethical implications of using data to predict future crimes based on past patterns. Ensuring that these algorithms are fair, unbiased, and transparent is crucial to preventing the perpetuation of existing social inequalities and ensuring that predictive policing tools are used responsibly and ethically.

Cybercrime and the Digital Frontier

The rise of cybercrime has created new challenges for law enforcement. Cybercriminals operate across borders and utilize sophisticated technology to commit crimes, making it difficult to track and apprehend them. Law enforcement agencies are adapting to this new reality by investing in specialized cybercrime units, building partnerships with private sector technology companies, and collaborating with international law enforcement agencies. The fight against cybercrime requires a multi-faceted approach, encompassing technical expertise, intelligence gathering, and international cooperation.

The Role of Technology in Community Engagement

Technology is not only transforming how law enforcement operates internally but also how it interacts with the public. Social media platforms have become vital tools for communication, community outreach, and building relationships. Law enforcement agencies utilize these platforms to share information, solicit tips, and engage in dialogue with the public. Furthermore, mobile applications are being developed to provide citizens with easy access to police services, report crimes, and receive updates on community events and safety initiatives.

Ethical Considerations and the Future of Policing

The integration of technology into law enforcement presents both opportunities and challenges. It offers the potential to improve efficiency, effectiveness, and transparency but also necessitates careful consideration of ethical implications. The use of surveillance technology, data analysis, and artificial intelligence raises concerns about privacy, bias, and the potential for misuse. Ensuring that these technologies are used responsibly and ethically is paramount to maintaining public trust and safeguarding civil liberties.

The future of policing will undoubtedly be shaped by technology. New tools and techniques are constantly emerging, and law enforcement agencies must stay ahead of the curve in adapting to this rapidly evolving landscape. However, it is crucial to prioritize ethical considerations, ensuring that technology is used to serve the public interest, promote transparency, and protect individual rights. The

challenge lies in striking a balance between harnessing the power of technology to enhance public safety and safeguarding the fundamental values of justice and fairness in the digital age.

The Promise and Peril of Artificial Intelligence

The integration of artificial intelligence (AI) into law enforcement represents a pivotal moment in the evolution of public safety. AI promises to revolutionize policing with its ability to analyze vast datasets, predict crime patterns, and optimize resource allocation. However, this technological advancement comes with significant ethical and practical considerations, raising concerns about potential biases, privacy violations, and the erosion of human judgment.

One of the most promising applications of AI in policing lies in crime prediction. By analyzing historical crime data, demographic patterns, and environmental factors, AI algorithms can identify areas at risk of criminal activity. This predictive capacity allows law enforcement agencies to proactively deploy resources, focusing on high-crime areas and potentially preventing crimes before they occur. Imagine a scenario where AI algorithms identify a surge in burglaries in a specific neighborhood due to a rise in unemployment or a recent influx of new residents. Based on this data, police could increase patrols, community outreach programs, or even implement targeted crime prevention strategies.

However, the potential benefits of AI-powered crime prediction must be weighed against the risks. Critics argue that these algorithms could perpetuate existing racial and socioeconomic biases within the justice system. If the data used to train AI models reflects historical disparities, the algorithms could potentially label certain communities as "high-risk" simply because they have been disproportionately targeted by law enforcement in the past. This could lead to over-policing of minority neighborhoods and a further widening of the racial gap in criminal justice.

Furthermore, the use of AI for crime prediction raises complex questions about privacy and civil liberties. Data collection and analysis for crime prediction often involve the collection of personal information, including location data, social media activity, and even financial records. If this data is not handled responsibly, it could be used to unfairly target individuals based on their personal characteristics, potentially leading to discrimination and even wrongful arrests.

Another area where AI is making significant inroads in policing is risk assessment. AI algorithms can analyze individual characteristics, such as criminal history, employment status, and social connections, to assess an individual's likelihood of committing future crimes. This information can be used by judges and parole boards to make decisions about bail, sentencing, and parole eligibility.

The promise of AI-driven risk assessment is to improve fairness and objectivity in the justice system. By relying on data-driven algorithms, the risk assessment process could potentially be less prone to human biases, which can play a significant role in sentencing disparities and the over-incarceration of certain populations. For example, an AI-powered risk assessment tool could help to reduce the likelihood that judges impose harsher sentences on individuals simply because they belong to a particular race or socioeconomic background.

However, the use of AI in risk assessment also carries substantial risks. Critics point out that these algorithms often rely on data that reflects historical biases, potentially leading to discriminatory outcomes. If the data used to train AI models reflects past patterns of racial and socioeconomic disparity in the justice system, the algorithms could perpetuate these inequalities by assigning higher risk scores to individuals from marginalized communities.

Furthermore, the use of AI in risk assessment raises ethical questions about the right to due process and the presumption of innocence. Relying on algorithms to assess an individual's likelihood of committing future crimes can be problematic if it undermines the fundamental principle of judging individuals based on their individual actions rather than on their potential for future wrongdoing.

Beyond crime prediction and risk assessment, AI is increasingly being used for resource allocation in law enforcement. AI algorithms can analyze crime data, traffic patterns, and other relevant factors to identify areas where police resources are most needed. This can help agencies to optimize their deployment of officers, allocate resources more efficiently, and improve response times to emergencies.

However, relying solely on AI algorithms for resource allocation can lead to unintended consequences. For example, an AI algorithm might identify a particular neighborhood as a low-crime area based on past crime data, but fail to account for emerging threats, such as a recent influx of drug activity or a rise in gang violence. This could lead to the under-policing of certain communities and the erosion of public safety.

Furthermore, the reliance on AI for resource allocation raises concerns about the potential for automation and the displacement of human officers. As AI technology becomes more sophisticated, it is possible that some routine law enforcement tasks, such as traffic enforcement and patrol duties, could be automated, potentially leading to job losses and a shift in the role of human officers.

It is crucial to approach the use of AI in law enforcement with caution and to consider the potential risks alongside the potential benefits. AI has the potential to revolutionize policing, but it is imperative to ensure that its implementation is guided by ethical principles, transparency, and accountability.

Here are some key considerations for the responsible development and deployment of AI in policing:

Data Bias and Fairness:

Law enforcement agencies must be vigilant about identifying and addressing potential biases in the data used to train AI algorithms. This includes ensuring that data reflects the diversity of the communities served and that it does not perpetuate historical inequalities.

Transparency and Accountability:

The use of AI in law enforcement should be transparent and accountable. The public must be informed about how AI is being used, the decisions being made based on AI algorithms, and the potential for bias. Law enforcement agencies must also be held accountable for the ethical use of AI technology.

Privacy and Civil Liberties:

The use of AI for surveillance and data collection must be balanced with the protection of individual privacy and civil liberties. Clear legal frameworks and oversight mechanisms are essential to ensure that AI technology is not used to infringe on fundamental rights.

Human Oversight and Judgment:

AI should not be used to replace human judgment altogether. It should be used as a tool to assist officers, provide insights, and enhance decision-making, but not to make decisions autonomously.

Public Engagement:

The development and deployment of AI in policing should involve meaningful public engagement to ensure that the technology is aligned with community values and priorities.

The integration of AI into law enforcement represents a significant shift in the landscape of public safety. While AI offers tremendous potential to improve efficiency, effectiveness, and fairness, its use must be guided by ethical principles, transparency, and a commitment to protecting civil liberties. By thoughtfully navigating the promise and peril of AI, law enforcement agencies can leverage its potential to enhance public safety while safeguarding the fundamental rights and freedoms of all citizens.

The Privacy Paradox

The rise of digital technology has fundamentally reshaped the landscape of law enforcement, bringing forth both incredible opportunities for enhancing public safety and significant concerns regarding individual privacy rights. This chapter examines the delicate balance between utilizing technology for public safety and protecting individual privacy rights in the digital age, delving into the complexities of this evolving paradox.

The advent of body cameras, surveillance systems, and data analysis tools has revolutionized the way law enforcement operates.

Body cameras, for instance, provide irrefutable visual evidence of interactions between officers and citizens, fostering transparency and accountability. Surveillance systems, ranging from traditional CCTV cameras to sophisticated facial recognition technology, can aid in crime prevention, investigation, and identifying suspects. Data analysis tools allow for identifying patterns and trends in crime data, enabling more effective allocation of resources and proactive policing strategies.

However, the use of such powerful technologies raises critical questions about privacy. Body cameras, while promoting transparency, can also capture sensitive information about individuals who are not involved in the incident being recorded. Surveillance systems, particularly facial recognition technology, can be misused for mass surveillance, leading to potential abuses and erosion of privacy. Data analysis tools, when used without proper safeguards, can perpetuate biases and lead to discriminatory policing practices.

The key challenge lies in finding a balance between harnessing the immense potential of technology for public safety while safeguarding individual privacy rights. This requires a nuanced approach that considers the following:

Transparency and accountability:

Implementing clear guidelines and regulations governing the use of technology in law enforcement, ensuring transparency and accountability in data collection, storage, and use.

Data privacy and security:

Implementing robust data protection measures to prevent unauthorized access, misuse, and breaches of sensitive information.

Algorithmic fairness and bias:

Addressing biases in algorithms used for crime prediction and risk assessment, ensuring that they do not perpetuate discrimination or unfairly target specific individuals or communities.

Public engagement and oversight:

Fostering open dialogue and active involvement of the public in shaping the use of technology in law enforcement, ensuring that their concerns are addressed and that technology is used ethically and responsibly.

The debate over the privacy paradox is ongoing and complex. Advocates for public safety argue that technology is essential for preventing crime, solving crimes, and protecting citizens. Conversely, privacy advocates argue that the use of technology without proper safeguards poses significant risks to individual freedoms and can lead to a surveillance society.

The future of law enforcement will undoubtedly be shaped by technological advancements. It is crucial to approach these advancements with a mindful and balanced perspective, prioritizing both public safety and individual privacy rights. This will require ongoing dialogue, collaboration, and a commitment to ethical and responsible use of technology. The success of this endeavor will ultimately determine the shape of our digital future, a future where the promise of technology is harnessed to create a safer and more just society while preserving the fundamental rights and freedoms of all citizens.

The following real-world examples illustrate the complexity of the privacy paradox:

The use of facial recognition technology:

While facial recognition technology can be effective in identifying suspects and tracking criminals, it has also been used for mass surveillance in some countries, raising concerns about its potential for abuse. The use of facial recognition technology for law enforcement purposes has become a hot topic of debate, with concerns about its potential for bias, discrimination, and the erosion of individual privacy.

The use of drones:

Drones can be valuable tools for surveillance, search and rescue operations, and even for monitoring crime scenes. However, there are concerns about their use for mass surveillance, potential for misuse, and invasion of privacy. The use of drones for law enforcement purposes has been met with mixed reactions, with some praising their potential benefits and others raising concerns about privacy violations.

The use of social media data:

Law enforcement agencies increasingly use social media data to gather information about suspects and potential threats. However, this practice raises concerns about the collection of personal data without consent, the potential for misuse, and the impact on individual privacy. The use of social media data by law enforcement is a complex issue with both potential benefits and risks.

These examples highlight the complex and evolving nature of the privacy paradox. As technology continues to advance, the need for robust safeguards to protect individual privacy rights while also ensuring the effective use of technology for public safety will only become more critical. The responsible and ethical use of technology in law enforcement will be essential in shaping a future where technology is a force for good, promoting both public safety and individual liberty.

The Future of Policing

The future of law enforcement is inextricably linked to the relentless evolution of technology. While technological advancements offer immense potential for innovation and efficiency, they also present significant challenges and ethical dilemmas that demand careful consideration. From the integration of artificial intelligence (AI) to the use of drones and facial recognition, the landscape of policing is undergoing a dramatic transformation, with far-reaching implications for both officers and the communities they serve.

One of the most significant technological advancements impacting law enforcement is the widespread adoption of artificial intelligence (AI). AI algorithms are being employed in various aspects of policing, including crime prediction, risk assessment, and resource allocation. Proponents argue that AI can help officers identify potential crime hotspots, allocate resources more effectively, and even predict individual criminal behavior, ultimately leading to a reduction in crime and improved public safety. For example, predictive policing systems analyze historical crime data to identify areas with a high probability of future offenses, allowing officers to focus their patrols and resources proactively.

However, the use of AI in law enforcement raises serious ethical concerns. Critics argue that AI algorithms can perpetuate and amplify existing biases, leading to unfair and discriminatory outcomes. For instance, if a predictive policing system is trained on data that reflects historical racial disparities in policing, it may generate predictions that disproportionately target individuals from minority communities. The potential for AI to perpetuate racial profiling and exacerbate existing inequalities is a critical issue that demands careful scrutiny and mitigation strategies.

Another emerging technology with profound implications for policing is the use of drones. Law enforcement agencies are increasingly utilizing drones for aerial surveillance, search and rescue operations, and even crime scene investigations. Drones offer a cost-effective and flexible alternative to traditional methods, providing officers with a bird's-eye view of a scene and access to areas that may be difficult or dangerous to reach. For example, drones equipped with thermal imaging cameras can be used to locate missing persons in rugged terrain or detect drug trafficking activities in remote locations.

However, the use of drones for surveillance purposes raises privacy concerns. The potential for drones to collect and store vast amounts of personal data without individual consent raises questions about the balance between public safety and individual privacy. Furthermore, the potential for drones to be misused for unauthorized surveillance or even weaponized poses a serious threat to civil liberties.

Facial recognition technology is another rapidly evolving technology with significant implications for law enforcement. Facial recognition systems use computer algorithms to identify individuals based on their facial features. Police departments are increasingly deploying facial recognition technology to identify suspects, track down missing persons, and even monitor crowds. For example, some cities are using facial recognition cameras in public spaces to identify individuals with outstanding warrants or to track suspicious behavior.

The use of facial recognition technology has sparked considerable debate about privacy and civil liberties. Critics argue that facial recognition systems can be inaccurate, prone to racial bias, and subject to misuse. In addition, the ability of facial recognition systems to track individuals in public spaces raises concerns about surveillance and government overreach. The potential for facial recognition technology to be used for mass surveillance or to monitor political dissent is a critical issue that requires careful ethical and legal considerations.

The evolving technological landscape presents law enforcement agencies with unprecedented opportunities to improve their efficiency, effectiveness, and responsiveness to community needs. However, it is crucial to recognize the potential pitfalls and ethical implications of these advancements. The adoption of new technologies must be accompanied by rigorous oversight, transparency, and accountability mechanisms to ensure that these tools are used ethically and responsibly.

As law enforcement agencies embrace new technologies, it is essential to prioritize the following key considerations:

Transparency and accountability:

Law enforcement agencies must be transparent about their use of technology, providing clear and understandable explanations of how these tools are being employed. Accountability mechanisms, such as independent oversight boards or audits, should be in place to ensure that technology is used fairly and ethically.

Privacy and civil liberties:

The use of technology must be balanced with respect for individual privacy and civil liberties. Clear legal frameworks and safeguards should be in place to prevent the misuse of technology for surveillance or harassment.

Bias and fairness:

AI algorithms and other technological tools should be designed and tested to minimize bias and ensure fairness. Law enforcement agencies should invest in training programs to help officers understand the potential biases of technology and the importance of critical thinking when using these tools.

Community engagement:

Law enforcement agencies should engage with their communities to solicit feedback and input on the use of technology. Transparency and open dialogue with the public are essential for building trust and legitimacy.

The future of policing is not simply about embracing the latest technology. It is about harnessing the power of innovation while ensuring that technology is used ethically and responsibly to enhance public safety and foster trust between law enforcement and the communities they serve. As technology continues to evolve, the challenge for law enforcement will be to find the right balance between embracing innovation and safeguarding civil liberties. This requires a commitment to ethical practices, transparency, and community engagement, ensuring that technological advancements are used to build a more just and equitable society.

Ethical Considerations

The rapid advancements in technology have undeniably reshaped the landscape of law enforcement, offering both exciting possibilities and profound ethical dilemmas. While technology can be a powerful tool for enhancing public safety, it's crucial to recognize the ethical considerations involved in its deployment. The responsible and accurate use of technology in law enforcement is paramount, demanding a commitment to accountability, transparency, and the protection of individual rights.

One of the most pressing ethical concerns is the potential for bias in algorithms and data analysis. Algorithms are often trained on historical data, which may reflect existing societal biases, leading to discriminatory outcomes. For instance, an algorithm designed to predict future crime based on past arrests might perpetuate racial disparities if historical arrest data reflects racial biases in policing practices. It's imperative to ensure that algorithms are developed and deployed with a critical eye to avoid perpetuating or amplifying existing biases.

The issue of privacy is another critical ethical consideration. The increasing use of surveillance technologies, such as body cameras, facial recognition systems, and drones, raises concerns about the erosion of privacy rights. While these technologies can enhance investigations and deter crime, they also have the potential to be misused or to infringe on the privacy of individuals who are not suspected of any wrongdoing. Striking a balance between public safety and individual privacy is a delicate task that requires careful consideration and robust legal frameworks.

Transparency is essential to maintaining public trust in law enforcement's use of technology. The public has a right to know how technology is being used, how data is being collected and analyzed, and what safeguards are in place to protect privacy. This transparency builds trust and accountability, reducing the likelihood of misuse or abuse.

Accountability for the use of technology in law enforcement is another critical element. Clear guidelines and procedures must be in place to govern the use of these tools, ensuring that they are used ethically and legally. Independent oversight bodies, such as civilian review boards, can play a vital role in ensuring accountability, investigating allegations of misconduct, and promoting transparency.

The ethical use of technology in law enforcement also requires a commitment to continuous learning and improvement. As technology evolves, so too must our understanding of its implications for public safety and individual rights.

Law enforcement agencies must invest in ongoing training and education for officers on the ethical and legal considerations of using technology, fostering a culture of responsible use.

Furthermore, the adoption of technology in law enforcement should not be seen as a replacement for traditional policing methods. Human interaction and community engagement remain critical components of effective policing. Technology should be viewed as a tool to augment, not replace, these essential aspects of law enforcement.

In conclusion, the ethical considerations of using technology in law enforcement are complex and multifaceted. A commitment to accountability, transparency, and the responsible use of data and algorithms is essential to ensuring that technology serves its intended purpose of enhancing public safety while protecting individual rights. By embracing ethical practices and fostering open dialogue with the public, law enforcement can leverage the power of technology to build safer and more just communities.

Chapter 9: The Community Connection: Building Trust and Fostering Relationships

The Importance of Community Engagement

Community engagement is not just a buzzword; it's the cornerstone of effective and sustainable policing. When law enforcement actively connects with the communities they serve, it fosters trust, builds relationships, and promotes positive interactions. This isn't about simply being "present" in the community but rather about actively listening, understanding, and working together to address shared concerns. It's about breaking down the barriers that often exist between officers and the public, creating a space for open dialogue, and fostering a sense of partnership.

Imagine a community where officers are seen as partners, not adversaries. Where residents feel comfortable approaching officers with concerns, seeking assistance, or simply sharing information. This is the ideal environment that community engagement seeks to create. The benefits of this proactive approach are manifold. First and foremost, it cultivates trust. When officers take the time to listen to community concerns, build relationships with local leaders, and participate in community events, they show genuine interest in the well-being of the people they serve. This fosters a sense of respect and understanding, building a foundation of trust that is essential for effective law enforcement.

Building relationships goes beyond simply establishing trust. It's about creating a network of support, where officers and community members work together to address issues, identify solutions, and build a safer environment for everyone. This can involve a range of activities, such as community policing initiatives, youth outreach programs, and collaborative crime prevention strategies. By working hand-in-hand, officers and community members gain a deeper understanding of each other's perspectives, concerns, and needs, paving the way for more effective and sustainable solutions.

Beyond building trust and relationships, community engagement also promotes positive interactions. When officers are seen as active participants in the community, not just as enforcers of the law, it helps to shift the perception of law enforcement from adversarial to collaborative. It creates opportunities for positive interactions, fostering a sense of shared responsibility for public safety and community well-being.

This type of engagement can take many forms. It could be a simple conversation with a resident during a routine patrol, attending a community meeting to listen to concerns, or participating in a local event. It could also involve more structured initiatives, such as youth mentoring programs, crime prevention workshops, or neighborhood watch groups. The key is to be proactive, to seek out opportunities to connect with the community, and to demonstrate a genuine commitment to building positive relationships.

The importance of community engagement cannot be overstated. It's about more than just public relations; it's about building a safer and more resilient society. When law enforcement actively engages with the communities they serve, it creates a space for dialogue, fosters trust, and promotes positive interactions. It helps to break down barriers, bridge divides, and ultimately build a safer and more equitable future for everyone.

One compelling example of the power of community engagement is the story of Officer John Smith (name changed for privacy), a veteran officer in a large metropolitan city. He recognized the disconnect between his department and certain minority communities, specifically those with a history of distrust and fear of police. Officer Smith realized that traditional law enforcement strategies were failing to bridge this gap. He proposed a community policing program that focused on building relationships with youth, especially those at risk of being drawn into criminal activities. He envisioned a program that went beyond simply enforcing the law, aiming to build trust, provide mentorship, and offer opportunities for positive growth.

The program, initially met with skepticism from some within the department, received enthusiastic support from community leaders and parents. Officer Smith, along with a small team of dedicated officers, initiated a series of outreach activities. They organized sports events, educational workshops, and mentoring sessions, connecting with young people on their own terms. They created a safe space for dialogue, listening to concerns, and offering guidance.

Over time, the program's impact became evident. The trust between officers and young people grew. There were tangible results too – a reduction in crime rates, improved communication, and a sense of shared responsibility for community safety. Officer Smith's initiative became a blueprint for similar programs within the department, demonstrating the power of community engagement in building trust, fostering positive relationships, and creating a safer environment for everyone.

While Officer Smith's story is inspiring, it's important to remember that building trust and fostering positive relationships with communities is an ongoing process. It requires constant effort, dedication, and a genuine commitment to understanding and serving the needs of the people. It's about being present in the community, not just in uniform but in heart and mind, recognizing that true safety comes from shared responsibility and a sense of belonging.

The Power of Dialogue

The foundation of trust, and ultimately, of a safe and harmonious society, rests upon open communication. For law enforcement officers, the ability to communicate effectively with the communities they serve is not just a skill; it's a necessity. This means building bridges, not walls, by engaging in genuine dialogue, actively listening to concerns, and fostering mutual understanding.

Think of it as a two-way street: Officers need to understand the concerns, fears, and experiences of the community, while members of the community need to understand the challenges, motivations, and limitations of law enforcement. Open communication, devoid of judgment and infused with empathy, is the key to bridging this gap.

Imagine a community meeting where a group of residents expresses their frustration about a recent increase in petty thefts. Instead of reacting defensively, the officer leading the meeting takes a deep breath and acknowledges the concerns, saying, "I hear your frustration, and I want to assure you that we're taking this seriously. We're actively investigating these incidents and exploring ways to enhance security measures in the area."

This simple act of validation, of actively listening and showing empathy, can go a long way in building trust. It demonstrates that the officer is genuinely concerned about the well-being of the community and is actively working to address their issues.

Active listening is more than just hearing words; it's about understanding the underlying emotions and perspectives. It's about asking clarifying questions, showing genuine interest in the community's experiences, and demonstrating respect for their viewpoints, even if they differ from your own.

For example, imagine a young officer responding to a domestic disturbance call. The officer might be inclined to jump straight into the situation, focusing on the immediate safety of those involved. However, if the officer takes a moment to listen to the individuals involved, they might discover a deeper issue that needs to be addressed, such as a history of domestic violence or a lack of access to resources.

Active listening allows officers to gather information, understand the root causes of conflict, and develop solutions that are tailored to the specific needs of the situation. It's about moving beyond reactive responses and adopting a more proactive approach to community safety.

Building trust takes time, effort, and consistent commitment. It requires officers to be approachable, accessible, and invested in their communities. They need to be willing to engage in dialogue, even when it's uncomfortable, and to be open to feedback, even if it's critical.

Think of the role of the "community police officer," who is assigned to a specific neighborhood and becomes a familiar face, a point of contact for residents, and a bridge between the police department and the community. This role requires officers to be proactive in building relationships, attending local events, and participating in community activities. They are expected to be visible, accessible, and invested in the well-being of the neighborhood.

But the power of dialogue doesn't stop at the level of individual officers. It extends to the entire law enforcement agency. Police departments need to prioritize open communication with the community, creating opportunities for feedback, dialogue, and partnership. This might involve:

Community forums:

Holding regular community meetings to address concerns, provide updates on investigations, and gather input from residents.

Youth engagement programs:

Developing programs that connect with young people, building positive relationships, and addressing issues of youth crime and violence.

Cultural sensitivity training:

Ensuring that officers are trained to understand the diverse cultural backgrounds and experiences of the communities they serve, promoting sensitivity and respect.

Transparency and accountability:

Being open and transparent about the work of the police department, sharing information about investigations, and being accountable for their actions.

Remember, the goal of law enforcement is to protect and serve the community. And this mission can only be truly successful when there is genuine trust, understanding, and collaboration between the police and the public. Open communication and active listening are not just tools for building relationships; they are essential building blocks for a safer, more just, and more harmonious society.

The Role of Education and Outreach

The Role of Education and Outreach: Educating the Public and Building Positive Perceptions

Building trust between law enforcement and the communities they serve is a multifaceted endeavor, and a crucial component of that effort lies in education and outreach. By engaging in proactive efforts to educate the public, law enforcement agencies can bridge the gap between perception and reality, fostering a more positive and understanding relationship.

The importance of education and outreach programs cannot be overstated. They serve as a bridge between the often-invisible world of law enforcement and the general public, dispelling misconceptions and promoting a more informed understanding of the profession's role in society. Such programs offer an opportunity to:

Debunk Myths and Misconceptions:

Media portrayals of law enforcement can often paint a distorted picture, perpetuating stereotypes and creating a disconnect between reality and public perception. Education and outreach programs provide a platform to address these misconceptions, offering factual information and insights into the complexities of police work. For instance, educational sessions can shed light on the delicate balance between enforcing the law and protecting individual rights, highlighting the challenges officers face in making split-second decisions in high-pressure situations. By addressing these misconceptions head-on, these programs help to bridge the gap between perception and reality.

Highlight the Human Element:

The image of law enforcement is often portrayed as a monolithic entity, overlooking the humanity of individual officers. Outreach programs can humanize the profession by showcasing the diverse experiences and motivations of those who choose to serve. Sharing personal stories of officers who dedicate their lives to public safety, showcasing their compassion, empathy, and commitment to justice, can foster a sense of connection and understanding. Engaging with the community through events like community policing initiatives, meet-and-greets, and educational workshops can humanize officers, demonstrating their dedication to serving and protecting their communities.

Promote Transparency and Accountability:

Building trust requires transparency and accountability. Education and outreach programs can be utilized to explain procedures, policies, and practices, fostering a sense of understanding about how law enforcement operates. By opening dialogue with the public, agencies can address concerns, receive feedback, and demonstrate their commitment to being responsive to community needs. This transparency can build trust by empowering citizens with knowledge and ensuring that they feel heard.

Foster Dialogue and Understanding:

These programs create a platform for constructive dialogue and exchange of perspectives. They provide opportunities for officers to engage with community members, listen to their concerns, and address their questions. This dialogue can help bridge cultural divides, break down barriers, and build a more inclusive and collaborative relationship between law enforcement and the community. Community forums, town hall meetings, and public forums can be effective tools for fostering this open dialogue, enabling citizens to voice their concerns, ask questions, and receive clear explanations from law enforcement officials.

Emphasize Collaboration and Partnership:

Building a strong community connection requires collaboration and partnership. Education and outreach programs can facilitate these collaborations by highlighting the importance of working together to address community issues and promote public safety. Partnerships with community organizations, schools, faith-based groups, and other local stakeholders can create a network of support and shared responsibility for improving public safety and building stronger communities. This shared responsibility strengthens community bonds and fosters a sense of collective ownership in addressing community challenges.

Successful education and outreach programs require careful planning, targeted messaging, and a commitment to continuous engagement. They should be designed to meet the specific needs and concerns of the communities they serve, tailored to different demographics and addressing relevant issues. The following are some key considerations for implementing effective outreach programs:

Targeted Messaging:

Tailoring messages to specific audiences is crucial. For example, programs aimed at youth might focus on building positive relationships with law enforcement, promoting responsible citizenship, and providing information about crime prevention. Programs geared towards senior citizens could address concerns about safety, scams, and fraud, offering resources and support.

Creative Engagement:

Engaging the community requires creativity and innovation. Traditional approaches like public presentations and brochures can be supplemented with more interactive methods such as social media campaigns, community events, and youth outreach programs.

Feedback and Evaluation:

Regularly assessing the effectiveness of outreach programs is essential for continuous improvement. Gathering feedback from community members, analyzing program participation, and evaluating outcomes help to identify areas for enhancement and ensure that programs remain relevant and impactful.

By investing in comprehensive education and outreach programs, law enforcement agencies can play a proactive role in fostering positive perceptions, building bridges of understanding, and creating a more collaborative and trust-based relationship with the communities they serve. This effort goes beyond simply enforcing the law; it's about building trust, fostering respect, and working together to create safer and more resilient communities for all.

The Importance of Diversity and Inclusion

The importance of diversity and inclusion within law enforcement cannot be overstated. It is not just about fulfilling quotas or ticking boxes; it is about building trust, fostering understanding, and ultimately, ensuring effective policing. A diverse law enforcement agency, one that reflects the demographics of the communities it serves, is a force for good. It fosters trust and legitimacy because community members see themselves represented in the officers who protect them. This representation goes beyond mere appearance; it involves a diversity of experiences, backgrounds, and perspectives.

Imagine a community grappling with a rise in gang violence. Having officers who understand the complexities of gang culture, who can speak the language and relate to the struggles of marginalized youth, can make all the difference in building relationships, gathering intelligence, and preventing further violence. Similarly, having officers with language skills and cultural understanding can be invaluable in communities with significant immigrant populations. They can serve as bridges between law enforcement and newcomers, promoting trust and facilitating communication.

However, diversity alone is not enough. Inclusion is equally crucial. It means creating a welcoming and supportive environment for officers from all backgrounds. This includes ensuring equal opportunities for advancement, addressing implicit bias in training and hiring practices, and promoting a culture of respect and inclusivity.

A truly inclusive law enforcement agency actively combats the unconscious biases that can permeate police work. It provides officers with comprehensive training on cultural competency, implicit bias, and de-escalation techniques. It emphasizes communication and active listening, recognizing that building trust requires genuine understanding and empathy.

The benefits of diversity and inclusion in law enforcement are manifold. A diverse force is better equipped to handle the complexities of a multicultural society. Officers with diverse backgrounds can better understand and respond to the needs of marginalized communities, reducing disparities in policing outcomes. It fosters a culture of empathy and respect, bridging the gap between law enforcement and the communities they serve. This, in turn, strengthens community relationships, facilitates the exchange of information, and ultimately, helps to reduce crime.

However, the path to achieving true diversity and inclusion in law enforcement is not without its challenges. Existing systemic barriers, such as implicit bias in hiring practices, lack of representation in leadership positions, and the historical legacy of racial profiling and police brutality, must be actively addressed.

The fight for diversity and inclusion in law enforcement is a long-term commitment. It requires a collective effort from law enforcement agencies, policymakers, and community members. It means investing in training, mentorship, and recruitment programs that actively seek out and support diverse candidates. It means holding police officers accountable for their actions and ensuring transparency in their operations.

Ultimately, the goal is to create a law enforcement system that is truly representative of the communities it serves, one that is built on trust, understanding, and mutual respect. This is not simply a matter of fairness and social justice; it is essential for the effectiveness and legitimacy of policing in a diverse and complex society.

Here are some examples of how diversity and inclusion can translate into tangible benefits:

Improved Community Relations:

A diverse police force can build stronger relationships with minority communities, fostering trust and encouraging cooperation.

More Effective Crime Prevention:

Officers from diverse backgrounds can better understand the root causes of crime in specific communities, leading to more effective crime prevention strategies.

Reduced Bias in Policing:

A diverse force can help reduce bias in policing by providing different perspectives and challenging preconceived notions.

Increased Transparency and Accountability:

A diverse police force can contribute to increased transparency and accountability by reflecting the values and concerns of the community.

Better Communication and Cultural Understanding:

Officers from diverse backgrounds can better communicate with people from different cultures, improving understanding and fostering trust.

Real-World Examples:

The New York City Police Department (NYPD):

The NYPD has made significant efforts to increase diversity and inclusion in its ranks, with positive results. The department has seen a decline in racial disparities in arrests and use of force since implementing reforms aimed at promoting diversity and cultural competency.

The Los Angeles Police Department (LAPD):

The LAPD has also focused on diversifying its ranks, with a particular emphasis on recruiting officers from minority communities. This has helped to build trust and improve community relations in Los Angeles.

The Oakland Police Department (OPD):

The OPD has implemented a number of programs to address implicit bias and promote cultural competency among its officers. These programs have been credited with reducing racial disparities in arrests and improving community trust.

While these are just a few examples, they demonstrate the positive impact of diversity and inclusion on law enforcement. It is essential that law enforcement agencies across the country continue to prioritize these values in order to build a more just and equitable society.

Furthermore, promoting diversity and inclusion in law enforcement is not just about numbers; it is about creating a culture of respect and understanding. This means:

Building a Culture of Empathy:

Training officers to understand and respond to the needs of diverse communities, particularly those who are marginalized or vulnerable.

Addressing Implicit Bias:

Providing training on implicit bias and de-escalation techniques to help officers recognize and mitigate their unconscious biases.

Creating Inclusive Leadership:

Encouraging and promoting diverse leadership within law enforcement to ensure that all voices are heard and valued.

Fostering Open Communication:

Promoting dialogue and communication between law enforcement and the communities they serve to build trust and understanding.

The journey toward a more diverse and inclusive law enforcement system is an ongoing process. It requires ongoing effort and commitment from all stakeholders. It is about creating a police force that is not just representative of the communities it serves, but one that is actively committed to serving those communities with fairness, justice, and respect.

Conclusion:

Diversity and inclusion in law enforcement are not just ideals; they are essential components of a just and effective policing system. A diverse and inclusive police force is better equipped to understand and respond to the complexities of a multicultural society, building trust, fostering understanding, and ultimately, ensuring that everyone is protected equally under the law. It is a journey that requires sustained effort and commitment, but the rewards of a more just and equitable society are well worth the journey.

The Future of Community Policing

The future of community policing lies in forging strong, collaborative partnerships between law enforcement agencies and the communities they serve. This shift from a traditional, top-down approach to a more collaborative model is essential for building safer, more resilient communities. To truly achieve this, we must move beyond reactive policing and focus on proactive strategies that address the root causes of crime and enhance public trust.

One of the key pillars of this future is fostering genuine dialogue and transparency. Law enforcement agencies need to actively engage with community members, listen to their concerns, and address their grievances with empathy and understanding. This means creating platforms for open communication, organizing community forums, and encouraging residents to share their perspectives on policing practices. Transparency is also paramount. Agencies should proactively release information about their policies, procedures, and performance data, fostering greater accountability and building public trust.

The future of community policing also necessitates a deeper understanding of the social determinants of crime. This means acknowledging that crime often stems from systemic inequalities, poverty, lack of opportunity, and social marginalization. Law enforcement agencies must partner with community organizations, social service providers, and educators to address these underlying issues, implementing programs that promote economic development, social justice, and educational opportunities. By tackling the root causes of crime, we can create safer communities that are less susceptible to criminal activity.

Furthermore, community policing necessitates a focus on crime prevention rather than simply reacting to incidents. This involves building partnerships with community members to identify and address potential risks before they escalate into crime. This might include organizing neighborhood watch programs, implementing crime prevention strategies in schools, and providing resources to at-risk individuals and families. By proactively working together, we can prevent crime before it happens, creating a safer environment for all.

Building a future where law enforcement and communities are partners in safety requires a commitment to diversity, inclusion, and representation within law enforcement agencies. By actively recruiting and promoting officers who reflect the diversity of the communities they serve, we can build trust and understanding. This means focusing on cultural sensitivity training, encouraging community policing initiatives led by officers from diverse backgrounds, and creating a more inclusive and welcoming environment for all officers.

Ultimately, the future of community policing is about building a shared vision for safety and well-being. It's about recognizing that law enforcement is a vital part of the community, not separate from it. By working together, embracing transparency, addressing root causes, and prioritizing prevention, we can create a future where communities are safer, more resilient, and where trust and understanding prevail.

Chapter 10: The Legacy of Service: Looking Back and Moving Forward

The Impact of Law Enforcement

The impact of law enforcement on society is undeniable, often overlooked, and extends far beyond the immediate response to emergencies and the apprehension of criminals. It's a force that shapes our daily lives, providing a sense of security and order that allows us to go about our days without fear of undue harm. The presence of law enforcement acts as a deterrent to crime, discouraging individuals from engaging in unlawful activities, knowing that there are consequences for their actions.

Think about the peace of mind we experience when we see a patrol car driving by our neighborhood, or the reassurance we feel when we call upon their assistance in a moment of crisis. These actions contribute to a feeling of safety, allowing individuals to focus on their lives, knowing they have a protective force behind them.

Beyond crime prevention, law enforcement plays a crucial role in protecting citizens from harm. They are the first responders to accidents, natural disasters, and other emergencies, providing immediate assistance and safeguarding the well-being of those involved. They also play a vital role in protecting vulnerable populations, such as children, the elderly, and victims of domestic violence, ensuring their safety and providing them with a lifeline in times of need.

One of the most fundamental contributions of law enforcement is the upholding of the rule of law. They are the guardians of our legal system, ensuring that laws are enforced fairly and impartially, and that justice is served. This role is essential for a functioning democracy, as it provides a foundation for social order, protects individual rights, and prevents the descent into chaos.

Furthermore, law enforcement plays a vital role in fostering community trust and cohesion. Officers who actively engage with their communities, building relationships and participating in local events, create a sense of partnership and understanding. This connection not only strengthens the bond between the police and the public but also fosters a more cooperative environment where citizens feel empowered to report crimes and collaborate with law enforcement.

However, it's crucial to acknowledge the challenges and complexities that law enforcement faces in a constantly evolving society. Issues of racial bias, police brutality, and excessive force have marred the profession's reputation and eroded trust in certain communities. It's important to recognize these challenges and work towards solutions that ensure accountability, transparency, and equal justice for all.

Despite the challenges, the positive contributions of law enforcement to society are immense. They are a critical pillar of our nation, providing safety, security, and the foundation for a just and equitable society. As we move forward, it's essential to recognize the sacrifices made by law enforcement officers, support their efforts to serve and protect, and work together to build a more just and safer world for all.

Examples of the positive impact of law enforcement can be seen in various aspects of our lives:

Crime prevention:

The presence of patrol cars, community policing programs, and proactive crime prevention initiatives deter criminal activity and create safer neighborhoods.

Citizen protection:

In situations of domestic violence, officers provide a safe haven for victims and apprehend abusers, preventing further harm. They are also vital in assisting victims of accidents, fires, and natural disasters, providing immediate aid and support.

Upholding the rule of law:

Police officers enforce traffic laws, investigate crimes, and apprehend criminals, ensuring that laws are followed and justice is served. This protects individual rights, maintains social order, and promotes a sense of fairness.

Community engagement:

Police officers participate in community events, build relationships with local residents, and engage in dialogue to address concerns and foster a sense of trust and cooperation.

The role of law enforcement is multifaceted and crucial to the well-being of society. Their dedication to upholding the law, protecting citizens, and fostering community trust contributes significantly to the quality of life we enjoy. It is vital to recognize and appreciate their sacrifices, support their efforts, and work together to address the challenges they face to ensure a safer and more just future.

The Stories of Resilience

The stories of resilience within the law enforcement community are as numerous as the officers themselves. Each day, officers face situations that test their courage, their commitment, and their very humanity. They encounter violence, confront despair, and witness the fragility of life. Yet, amidst the darkness, their dedication to serving others shines through, illuminating the path toward a safer and more just society.

One such story of resilience is that of Officer Jones, a veteran patrol officer in a large metropolitan city. Having witnessed countless acts of brutality and suffering during her years on the force, Officer Jones had developed a deep empathy for victims of crime. She was known throughout her precinct for her compassion and her unwavering commitment to helping those in need.

One particularly harrowing incident that tested Officer Jones' resilience involved a domestic violence call. Arriving at the scene, she found a young woman visibly shaken, her face marred by bruises. The woman's partner, enraged and drunk, had subjected her to a violent assault. Officer Jones immediately apprehended the attacker, calming the situation and ensuring the woman's safety. She later took the woman to a local hospital, where she stayed with her until a crisis counselor arrived. This unwavering support and kindness exemplified Officer Jones' dedication to protecting victims and advocating for their well-being.

The emotional toll of this incident, however, was significant. Despite the overwhelming stress and trauma, Sarah refused to let it break her. She sought support from colleagues, confided in her family, and sought counseling to help process the emotional weight she was carrying. Her resilience and commitment to her calling were a testament to the strength of character that many officers possess.

Another story of resilience comes from Detective Thompson, an investigator who spent years dedicated to uncovering the truth in complex cases. Detective Thompson's job often required him to delve into the darkest corners of human nature, encountering deception, corruption, and acts of brutality. He was known for his meticulous attention to detail, his unwavering pursuit of justice, and his unwavering commitment to helping victims find closure.

One case that particularly tested Detective Thompson's resilience involved the investigation of a serial killer who had terrorized the city for months. The case was fraught with emotional turmoil, as detective Thompson tirelessly interviewed families of victims, painstakingly collected evidence, and faced the overwhelming pressure of bringing a dangerous criminal to justice. He poured his heart and soul into the investigation, driven by a desire to bring peace to the families affected by the killer's heinous acts.

The toll of the investigation was immense, taking a heavy toll on Detective Thompson's personal life. He missed countless family events, sacrificed sleep, and dedicated himself to the case until it was finally solved. Detective Thompson's resilience was not only in his ability to face the darkness but also in his unwavering commitment to finding justice for those who had been wronged.

These stories are not isolated incidents. They are just two examples of the countless acts of resilience and dedication displayed by law enforcement officers across the country. Each day, these officers confront the challenges of their profession with courage, compassion, and an unwavering commitment to serving their communities. Their sacrifices and their strength are a testament to the human spirit and the power of service.

Beyond their individual stories, the collective resilience of law enforcement officers is a powerful force. They form a brotherhood and sisterhood, bonded by their shared experiences, their unwavering commitment to upholding the law, and their dedication to protecting those in need. This bond provides them with a sense of community, a source of strength, and a support system in times of need.

The resilience of officers is not solely an individual characteristic but a product of the shared culture and values within law enforcement. They are trained to confront danger, to maintain composure under pressure, and to persevere in the face of adversity. This collective resilience, honed through rigorous training and shared experiences, allows them to withstand the mental and emotional challenges of the job.

The resilience of law enforcement officers is also shaped by their belief in the importance of their mission. They understand that their work is not just a job; it is a calling, a responsibility to protect their communities and uphold the rule of law. This belief in the greater good, in the importance of justice, and in the need for order provides them with the strength to continue serving despite the hardships they face.

The stories of resilience among law enforcement officers are a testament to the unwavering spirit of those who dedicate their lives to serving others. They are a reminder that even in the darkest of times, there is hope, strength, and the enduring power of the human spirit. Their courage, their commitment, and their unwavering dedication to justice are a source of inspiration and a testament to the importance of service.

However, it is crucial to acknowledge that while resilience is essential, it is not a substitute for adequate support systems. Officers need access to mental health resources, support networks, and opportunities to process the trauma they experience. They need to be recognized for their sacrifices, their dedication, and the emotional burden they carry.

As we celebrate the stories of resilience within law enforcement, we must also recognize the need for change and improvement. The demands of the job can be overwhelming, and officers need to be provided with the tools and resources to maintain their well-being. This includes prioritizing mental health, promoting a culture of support, and addressing the systemic challenges that contribute to the burdens officers face.

The stories of resilience within law enforcement are a call to action. It is a call to acknowledge the sacrifices officers make, to support their mental well-being, and to work together to create a safer and more just society.

As we move forward, let us remember the courage, the compassion, and the unwavering dedication of those who stand on the thin blue line, protecting our communities and upholding the rule of law. Their stories are a reminder of the enduring power of the human spirit and the importance of service.

The Future of the Profession

The future of law enforcement is not etched in stone; it's a canvas waiting to be painted. The 21st century is a dynamic landscape, teeming with challenges and opportunities, and policing must evolve to meet them. Embracing change, fostering innovation, and adapting to the evolving needs of society are not just options, but necessities for the profession to thrive.

Gone are the days of rigid, hierarchical structures, where information flowed from the top down and innovation was stifled. Instead, the future demands a collaborative, community-oriented approach. Officers must become problem-solvers, not just responders. They must actively engage with the communities they serve, understanding their concerns, their needs, and their perspectives. This shift requires building trust, fostering dialogue, and breaking down the barriers that have historically separated law enforcement from the public.

Technology is transforming the landscape of policing, offering both tremendous opportunities and complex challenges. Body cameras have become standard, promoting transparency and accountability. Data analytics and artificial intelligence are being used to predict crime patterns and allocate resources more effectively. Drones are employed for surveillance and crime scene investigations. While these advancements hold immense potential, they raise critical questions about privacy, bias, and ethical use.

A key concern is the potential for algorithmic bias in AI-driven policing. If algorithms are trained on data that reflects historical biases, they may perpetuate those biases, leading to discriminatory outcomes. This issue demands careful consideration and ethical safeguards to ensure fairness and equity.

The future of policing also necessitates a renewed focus on de-escalation, crisis intervention, and mental health awareness. Officers are increasingly called upon to address situations involving individuals experiencing mental health crises, substance abuse, or other vulnerabilities. Training in de-escalation techniques, understanding the impact of trauma on behavior, and collaborating with mental health professionals will become crucial.

As the world becomes increasingly interconnected, transnational crime and cybersecurity threats present new challenges. Law enforcement agencies will need to collaborate with each other and with international organizations to address these complex issues. Sharing information, intelligence, and best practices will be essential.

The future of law enforcement is not just about technology, but about human connection. Building trust with communities is fundamental to ensuring public safety and fostering a sense of shared responsibility. This means actively engaging in community dialogues, addressing concerns, and working collaboratively to find solutions.

The profession must also prioritize the well-being of its officers. Mental health support, robust training programs, and supportive work environments are essential to combat stress, trauma, and burnout. Recognizing and addressing the unique challenges faced by law enforcement officers is crucial to retaining and supporting a strong, ethical, and resilient workforce.

The future of law enforcement demands a paradigm shift. It's about moving from a reactive to a proactive approach, from a culture of isolation to one of collaboration, and from a focus on punishment to one of rehabilitation. It's about embracing technology responsibly, fostering trust with communities, and prioritizing the well-being of officers. It's about a future where law enforcement is not just a force, but a force for good, working hand-in-hand with the communities it serves to create a safer and more just society. This is the future that we must strive for, a future where the badge represents not just power, but service, compassion, and an unwavering commitment to protecting and serving all.

The Call to Action

The legacy of service that law enforcement officers leave behind extends far beyond their years on the job. They leave a mark on the communities they serve, a tangible impact on the safety and well-being of countless individuals. Their unwavering dedication to upholding the law, protecting the innocent, and serving the public interest shapes the very fabric of our society.

It is crucial that we, as citizens, acknowledge and appreciate the sacrifices they make. These sacrifices are not merely confined to the dangerous situations they encounter daily; they extend to their personal lives, their relationships, and their overall well-being. The emotional toll of witnessing trauma, the financial burdens of the profession, and the constant pressure to maintain a stoic facade take their toll. Yet, they continue to answer the call, to rise to the challenges, and to confront danger head-on.

One way to demonstrate our support and appreciation is through simple acts of kindness. A heartfelt thank you, a smile, or a gesture of encouragement can go a long way in reminding officers that their service is valued. We can also engage in positive dialogue and actively challenge negative stereotypes and prejudices. Instead of fueling the flames of mistrust and animosity, let us build bridges of understanding and compassion.

It is also essential to recognize the systemic challenges faced by law enforcement. We must advocate for fair compensation, comprehensive mental health support, and robust training programs that equip officers with the necessary tools to navigate the complexities of their profession. We can do this by engaging with our elected officials, participating in community dialogues, and supporting organizations that promote positive change within law enforcement.

The call to action is clear: Let us extend a hand of support to those who serve and protect us. Let us show our appreciation for their sacrifices and contribute to a more supportive and understanding environment. By working together, we can ensure that the legacy of service left behind by law enforcement officers is one of honor, respect, and positive impact.

We can also promote positive change by encouraging the recruitment of diverse individuals, fostering a culture of transparency and accountability, and supporting initiatives that promote community policing and collaborative problem-solving. By working together, we can build a stronger, safer, and more just society, one where the legacy of service is a source of pride and inspiration for generations to come.

The Legacy of Service

The legacy of service left by law enforcement officers extends far beyond their active years on the force. It's a lasting impact that ripples through communities and resonates across generations. Each officer, by choosing this path, becomes a part of a tapestry woven with threads of courage, dedication, and a profound commitment to safeguarding the well-being of others.

Think about the countless times officers have responded to emergencies, their presence a beacon of hope in moments of fear and chaos. They have faced down danger, calmed volatile situations, and brought comfort to those in need. Their actions, often taken in the face of adversity, have prevented crimes, protected innocent lives, and upheld the rule of law.

The stories of these officers, their acts of bravery and compassion, become part of the collective memory of their communities. They inspire a sense of security, a belief that justice will prevail. It's not just about the arrests made or the crimes solved; it's about the lives touched, the fears allayed, and the sense of order maintained.

Their legacy is also etched in the lives they have personally impacted. The families they have comforted, the children they have protected, the individuals whose lives they have saved – these are the lasting testaments to their service. Their commitment to duty has not only shaped their own lives but has left an indelible mark on the lives of countless others.

The legacy of service also extends to the future. It serves as a blueprint for the next generation of officers, inspiring them to embrace the challenges and rewards of this noble profession. It encourages them to uphold the highest standards of integrity, to treat all individuals with respect, and to always strive for justice.

But the legacy of service isn't just about the past; it's also about the future. It's about the ongoing pursuit of excellence, the constant striving to improve the profession, and the dedication to building stronger, safer communities.

This pursuit involves embracing change, adapting to new challenges, and finding innovative solutions. It means actively seeking ways to strengthen relationships with the communities served, fostering trust and understanding, and promoting transparency and accountability. It's about building a future where law enforcement is viewed as a force for good, a pillar of justice, and a protector of individual rights.

In the end, the legacy of service isn't just about what officers have accomplished; it's about what they continue to inspire. It's about the unwavering commitment to making a difference, to upholding the law, and to protecting the rights and freedoms of all. It's a legacy that continues to shape the world, one courageous act, one compassionate deed, and one unwavering commitment to serving others at a time.

Acknowledgment

This book would not have been possible without the support and encouragement of many individuals. I am deeply grateful to the law enforcement officers who bravely shared their personal stories and insights, allowing me to offer a glimpse into the often-overlooked realities of their profession. Their willingness to be vulnerable and transparent is a testament to their courage and commitment to service.

I extend my sincere thanks to the families and loved ones of law enforcement officers, whose unwavering support and understanding are essential to those who serve. Their sacrifices and resilience are equally inspiring.

I am also indebted to my colleagues in law enforcement, who have provided invaluable guidance and expertise throughout the writing process. Their knowledge and experience have greatly enriched this work.

Finally, I would like to express my gratitude to the countless individuals who have dedicated their lives to upholding the law and protecting our communities. Your service is a testament to the strength and resilience of the human spirit.

Appendix

This appendix provides supplementary materials for further exploration of the topics discussed in the book. It includes:

A comprehensive list of resources

for law enforcement officers, including mental health support organizations, financial literacy programs, and advocacy groups.

Statistics and data

on the challenges faced by law enforcement officers, such as salary disparities, mental health rates, and crime trends.

Examples of best practices

in community policing, transparency, and accountability in law enforcement.

Glossary

Blue Wall:

The culture of secrecy and loyalty among law enforcement officers, often creating barriers to accountability and transparency.

Community Policing:

A policing philosophy that emphasizes collaboration and engagement with the communities served, fostering trust and building positive relationships.

Implicit Bias:

Unconscious attitudes and stereotypes that can influence decision-making, often resulting in unintentional discrimination.

Post-Traumatic Stress Disorder (PTSD):

A mental health condition triggered by traumatic events, characterized by intrusive memories, avoidance behaviors, and emotional distress.

Shift Work Syndrome:

The negative physical and psychological effects of working irregular shifts and long hours, impacting sleep, relationships, and overall well-being.

References

Analysis / Case Study

Elizabeth Mullen & Linda J. Skitka (2006). Analyses Of Social Issues And Public Policy, An Analysis Of The Rodney King Case

Maggie Hadley (2022). Behind The Blue Wall Of Silence: Racial Disparities in The NYPD Discipline

Elizabeth J. Andonova . Cycle of Misconduct: How Chicago has Repeatedly Failed to Police its Police

Jessica Lussenhop (2018). Rogue Baltimore Police Unit Ringleader Wayne Jenkins Sentenced

Peter Bloom (2014). Eric Garner, The 'American Problem' And A Chance To Unite

Betsy Reed (2015). Discrimination in Ferguson: Full Extent Of Police Bias Laid Bare In Damning Report

Brandon Epstein, James Emerson, and ChatGPT (2024). "Navigating the Future of Policing: Artificial Intelligence

Government reports and statistics

Bureau Of Justice Statistics (2022). Contacts Between Police And The public, 2020

Bureau Of Justice Statistics (2022). Local Police Department Personnel, 2020

FBI.Gov (2024) Law Enforcement Officers Killed and Assaulted (LEOKA) Program

Books

Mathew B. Gordon (2011). The Thin Blue Line (Second Edition)

Edwin J. Delattre (2011). Character And Cops (Sixth Edition)

Matthew Horace & Ron Harris (2018). The Black And The Blue (First Edition)

Adam Davis (2018). Behind The Badge, 365 Daily Devotions For Law Enforcement

Kevin M. Gilmartin (2002). Emotional Survival For Law Enforcement: A Guide For Officers

James Patterson & Matt Eversmann (2023). Walk The Blue Line: They Walk The Line Between Life And Death

Allen R. Kates (1999). Cop Shock: Surviving Posttraumatic Stress Disorder (PTSD)

Terrence Hake & Wayne Klatt (2021). Operation Greylord

Author Biography

Sgt. Dustin Mayhue #1120

My journey into law enforcement began in 2014, but the seeds of this passion were sown long before that. At 32 years old, with six years of marriage to my beautiful wife, Brittany, and two incredible children, Sarah and Dustilynn, I found myself at a pivotal crossroads in life. My family means the world to me, and their support has been a cornerstone of my endeavor to pursue a career that I had dreamt about since I was 18 years old.

Growing up, I always felt a calling to serve and protect my community. While I did not have the opportunity to serve in the military—something I sometimes wish I had the chance to do—I knew that law enforcement was my true path. It was a conversation with Brittany that ignited the fire within me at the age of 31. I shared my desire to become a Police Officer, and her unwavering support and encouragement made it clear that I could turn this dream into a reality.

With her backing, I took decisive steps toward my goal. I enrolled in a Police Academy, a decision that transformed not only my life but also the lives of my family. Balancing my studies during the day with running my shop at night was no easy task. For six grueling months, I operated on just four hours of sleep, fueled by energy drinks and sheer determination. But I was committed; I was driven. I emerged from the academy in July 2014, ready to embark on this new chapter of my life.

In August of that same year, I officially started my career in law enforcement. Each day on the job has been a journey of growth and learning, filled with valuable experiences that have shaped me as an officer and as a person. I take immense pride in serving my community, working tirelessly to ensure safety and justice for all. With every challenge I face, I am reminded of the sacrifices my family continues to make and the support they provide.

I am passionate about building relationships within the community, fostering trust, and promoting cooperation between law enforcement and the citizens we serve. I believe that transparency and communication are essential to effective policing, and I strive to exemplify these values in every interaction I have.

As I continue on this path, I remain committed to personal and professional development, always seeking new ways to enhance my skills and better serve my community. My family remains my motivation, and their love drives me to be the best officer and person I can be. In every decision I make, every situation I handle, and every life I touch, I carry their support with me.

This is just the beginning of my journey in law enforcement. I look forward to the challenges ahead, knowing that each experience will contribute to my growth and the betterment of the community I serve. Thank you for taking the time to learn about my career and my commitment to making a difference.